D0055693

05/23
STRAND PRICE
$5.00

WEIRD AND WONDERFUL WORDS

nihilarian a person who deals with things of no importance (whether by choice or not is unclear).

WEIRD AND WONDERFUL WORDS

EDITED BY
Erin McKean

ILLUSTRATIONS BY
Roz Chast

WITH A FOREWORD BY SIMON WINCHESTER

OXFORD
UNIVERSITY PRESS
2002

OXFORD

UNIVERSITY PRESS

Oxford   New York

Auckland   Bangkok   Buenos Aires   Cape Town   Chennai
Dar es Salaam   Delhi   Hong Kong   Istanbul   Karachi   Kolkata
Kuala Lumpur   Madrid   Melbourne   Mexico City   Mumbai   Nairobi
São Paulo   Shanghai   Singapore   Taipei   Tokyo   Toronto

Copyright © 2003 by Oxford University Press, Inc.

Illustrations © by Roz Chast

Published by Oxford University Press, Inc.
198 Madison Avenue, New York, NY 10016-4314
http://www.oup.com

Oxford is a registered trademark of Oxford University Press

All rights reserved. No part of this publication may be reproduced,
stored in a retrieval system, or transmitted, in any form or by any means,
electronic, mechanical, photocopying, recording, or otherwise,
without the prior written permission of Oxford University Press.

Library of Congress Cataloging-in-Publication Data

Data available

Designed by Nora Wertz

Popeye (p. 3) is the property of King Features Syndicate

9 8 7 6 5 4 3 2 1

Printed in the United States of America
on acid-free paper

TABLE OF CONTENTS

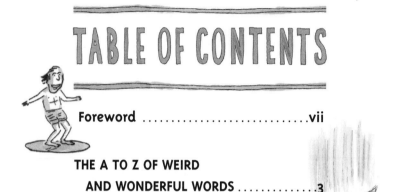

For
Joey and Henry

FOREWORD

Some years ago, at a time when I wrote a weekly column in a large daily London newspaper and thus vaingloriously fancied that I had some influence over popular taste, I invented a word. It was, I thought, a rather pretty-sounding word, though, I confess, not an overly attractive creation to see. It was the word *drimmens,* and it was the name that I conjured up (on a train, chuffing through the Cotswolds, while I looked out on fields of unsullied winter white) to signify the trail of gray water that is invariably left behind on the floor when someone in gumboots comes into a warm kitchen from the snowy outside world.

I still wonder how I came up with it. Perhaps I assumed I would be roundly cursed later that night for leaving such a trail when I arrived home from the station: I can't quite remember any other motive for inventing this two-syllable confection, and for vowing to include it in the next week's column, other than that I expected to leave a trail of drimmens behind me on my way to greet my wife.

It seemed a most straightforward, unfussy kind of word. The orthography was simple, the pronunciation was uncomplicated, and the etymology—while admittedly rather more whim-based than classically constructed—seemed pleasingly neat. I think, if I remember properly, that it was probably a loose mixture of *drip* and *midden* (the former suggesting wetness and cold, the latter dirt and grayness). It was in addition deliberately set in the permanent plural, since wet kitchen boots always leave behind a piecemeal trail rather than a single print. And it had the look and feel of Old English about it—such that friends on whom I tried it expected it not to be a neologism at all, but a word already lurking somewhere deep in the bowels of the *Oxford English Dictionary,* with a string of cited uses, probably sixteenth century, and coming from some striding and booted figures like Sir Francis Drake and Sir Philip Sidney.

But in fact it isn't to be found in the *OED,* or anywhere else. Moreover, and surprisingly, not only does *drimmens* not exist, but there is no word in English that begins with the four letters *drim,* however ancient the prefix sounds. There is nothing at all, in fact, to be found in any lexicon I have consulted between *drily* and *drink*—a gap appearing in all dictionaries that yearns to be filled. Hence have I now duly, and with the persuasive benefit of many months' worth of my newspaper column, done my level best to fill it.

All, however, to no avail. I shouldn't have bothered. The word does not now exist. No one liked it enough ever to use it. It never caught on. It can hardly be said to be dead since, in truth, it never lived. I have had to reel it pathetically back into its fold, while at the same time watching enviously as ugly homunculi of words like *yomp* and *J-Lo* and *new variant CJD* stagger out into the sunlight and begin to enjoy their own full and meaningful lives in the great and noble body of the English tongue. These and a score of others from our wretched times seem to me quite horrid words; mine, on the other hand, is cute. It all seems so blessedly unfair.

But I am comforted, in reading the pages that follow, with the knowledge that in my rejection I am in excellent company. "Not quite!" the pedantic will rightly cry—for the words that Erin McKean has assembled for our pleasure do technically exist, while my unloved singleton does not.

But in truth these hundreds that follow might just as well not exist either, since they are all now almost entirely unused, are by and large forgotten, and are nearly all in danger of being consigned to the same lexical scrap heap from which mine has not yet risen.

Yet what binds them to mine, I feel, is that these are all exceptionally *agreeable* words, pretty to look at and to hear, nice of definition, each a marvel of etymology and construction, and well worth saving and resurrecting. They are all to be described by a phrase that only exists in the French: they are *bons mots*, a gallimaufry of philological delights.

For who could not but love *tappen*, with which leafy plug a bear seals up his bottom for the winter; or *iotacist*, one who (see all above for a living example) indulges in excessive use of the letter *i*; or the word for that oft-encountered follower of the rural trade of horse-dissecting, a *hippotomist*; or the Scots word *waff*, which means just the *slightest touch* of illness.

Our language is a rich one indeed, the richest in creation, and a privilege to know. It is ever-changing, ever-expanding, with the current lexicon like an ever-rolling conveyor belt, moving words from invention to burial with langorous certitude. This collection of Erin McKean's pauses the belt for just a few seconds so that we may pluck from it some choice delights, and place them back at the beginning to enjoy for a while more.

Drimmens is not there, more's the pity. But *weesel* is, along with *pannage* and *choronym*, *angletwitch* and *empasm* and *elaqueate* and *dragoman* and some hundreds more—some of them weird, all of them wonderful, and English, every one. Read them, savor them—and once in a while, perhaps even make use of them—next time you glimpse the backside of a hibernating bear, maybe; or if you see a trail of melted snow upon a pristine kitchen floor.

—Simon Winchester

INTRODUCTION

What makes a word weird? It would be convenient to say that it's as ineffable as whatever it is that makes art Art, but that's not quite true. Words are weird because they have odd sounds, or an abundance of syllables, or a completely gratuitous *k, j, q, z,* or *x.* Words are often weird because they mean something weird. They let you see, for as long as you care to dwell on them, some of the truly bizarre things that people have had, done, used, invented, feared, or thought.

What makes a word wonderful *is* ineffable. It has to hit you like a good joke, or a satisfying denouement, or the scent of something tantalizing in the air. It makes you want to go off on tangents, or rants, or wild goose chases. It adds something, not just to your vocabulary (since you may never even speak or write any of these wonderful words), but to your being. Like anything wonderful (to abuse etymology), it fills you with wonder. It opens vistas.

I hope that by combining the weird with the wonderful (with wonderfully weird illustrations by Roz Chast, herself ineffable) in selecting these words we have made a book of vistas and not a linguistic freakshow. There are plenty of words that are weird without being the least bit wonderful—*nectocalyx* is orthographically weird, but meaning as it does 'the swimming-bell that forms the natatory organ in many hydrozoans' it is sadly lacking on the wonder scale. There are wonderful words, such as *brio* and *luminescent,* which long familiarity has deprived of any weirdness. Finding a truly weird and wonderful word is like meeting a gorgeous person who is also a good cook and will help you move.

Tremendous thanks and credit go to Sara Hawker and Angus Stevenson, whose original promotional booklet of weird and wonderful words for Oxford in the UK sparked the idea for this book, and also to Michael Quinion for much of the original material. Quite a few of the words within are from their personal collections, for which I am most grateful (it's lovely that you can give a word away and still keep it for your own). Thanks also to Martin Coleman, for managing the project, relative pronouns, bacon, and all; Sandra Ban, for keeping our quotation marks in line; Nora Wertz, for all things designed; and Casper Grathwohl, for perseverance, enthusiasm, and number-juggling.

WEIRD AND WONDERFUL WORDS

ALOGOTROPHY

aboulia the loss of will or volition, as a mental illness. It's related to a Greek word meaning 'thoughtlessness.'

agliff a verb only found in the past participle as *aglifft*, meaning 'frightened.' It is related to the equally obsolete *gliff*, meaning 'to alarm.'

agnate a relation by descent from a common male ancestor, especially on the father's side.

agonistarch a person who trained combatants for games. A much more intimidating word than our modern *coach*.

alexiteric an adjective meaning 'able to ward off contagion' or 'having the properties of an antidote.' Both rubber gloves and ipecac could be called *alexiteric*. This word comes from a Greek word meaning 'protection.'

alogotrophy excessive nutrition to any one part of the body, resulting in deformity. Like many unnerving and disturbing medical words, this one seems to be more a theory of disease than an actual condition. It comes from Greek roots meaning 'unreasonable nourishment.'

angletwitch (also *angletouch*) an obsolete but charming word meaning 'a worm used as bait in fishing.'

antapology a reply to an apology. Very rare, this word deserves a wider use to describe responses to apologies such as "Well, you should be sorry!"

ABERRANT AND AMAZING ANATOMY

Anyone who has ever contemplated

the essential humor of the belly button (*omphalodium*) or the big toe (*hallux*) would not be surprised at the number of unusual words available to describe our odd extremities and parts.

There are quite a few terms right at your fingertips. The very fingertip, the part with the fingernail, is the *metacondylus*. The fingertip, not including the nail, is the *dactylion*. The nail itself is an *unguicule*. Your *annularis*, or ring-finger, not only has a direct line to your heart, but supposedly also cures disease (thus the name *leech-finger* if you're a doctor). If you're all thumbs, perhaps you have one *pollex* too many? If you have lost a thumb, you're *murcous*. If you have one finger or toe too many (especially one on the far side of your little toe or little finger) it's a *postminimus*. Your little finger is also called your *ear-finger* or *auricular*, being the most convenient, one assumes, for investigations into the *souse*, 'ear.' The hollow of the external ear is called the *alveary*, because the wax is found there. *Alveary* comes from a Latin word meaning 'beehive.' The little flap on the inner side of the external ear is the *tragus*; it is opposite the *helix*, which is the rim of the external ear. The palm of the hand and the sole of the foot have the same name—*thenar*, which is also the name for the ball of muscle at the base of the thumb.

Your bendy parts also have good names. You may not know your ear from your *ancon* if you're unaware that your *ancon* is your elbow. The bend of the elbow itself is the *bought*. Your *oxter* is your armpit. *Knapper* for knee is a little easier to grasp, but most people don't know that the space behind the knee is called the *hough*. The kneecap has a slew of names, including *knop, rotula, rowel, shive, whirl-bone,* and *pattle-bone*. Something that bends like a knee is *geniculate*. Going from the top down on the leg, you can refer to your *coxa* or *huckle* (hip), *meros* (thigh), *hockshin* or *gambrel* (the underside of your thigh), *sparlire* (calf), *astragalus* or *coot* (ankle-bone), down to the *pterna* (heel-bone).

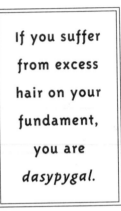

If you suffer from excess hair on your fundament, you are *dasypygal.*

If you're sitting down while you read this, you are using your *crupper, fud, bewscher, hurdies, crus, rass,* and *toute* to its full potential, not to mention your *crena*, 'the crease between the buttocks.' (If you suffer from excess hair on your fundament, you are *dasypygal*.)

There are all sorts of little odds and ends around the body that have good names, like the *columella*, the little flap that hangs down in the back of your throat (often called the *uvula*), and the cavity in which it hangs, the *fauces*. The blank spaces of your face, like the *glabella* (the space between your eyebrows) and the *philtrum* or *pallium* (the dent of your upper lip) should be, in most cases, *glabrous* 'smooth.' It sounds more determined to grit your *mompyns* instead of your teeth, or to stick out your *pogonion* 'most projecting part of a chin.' Quite possibly the nicest term of all, though, is *heart-spoon*, the little dent at the end of your sternum. Or it would be, if the citations for it didn't involve it being used to whet an attacker's knife.

apocatastatis the return to a previous condition. Although mostly used in astronomical and medical contexts, this would make a nice alternative to the overused *rehab*. "We've almost completed our *apocatastatis*; we're just waiting for the tiles we ordered from Italy."

apocrisiary a person appointed to give answers. Used especially of papal nuncios, this word has a much nicer (and more impressive sound) than *Public Relations Manager*. It comes from a Greek word meaning 'answer.'

apoptosis the death of cells which occurs as a normal part of an organism's growth or development: a less technical term for this process is *programmed cell death*. The term *apoptosis* comes from Greek, in which it means 'falling-off.'

aprosexia an abnormal inability to pay attention, characterized by near-complete indifference to everything (as opposed to generic, run-of-the-mill absent-mindedness). It is contrasted with *hyperprosexia*, concentration on one thing to the exclusion of everything else, and *paraprosexia*, the inability to pay attention to any one thing, caused by a constant state of distraction.

aquamanile a bowl or jug made in the form of an animal or bird.

argute an adjective meaning 'shrewd.' Arising in the sixteenth century from a Latin word meaning 'clear or sharp,' it is a very rare word used only in scholarly or literary writing.

aristotle Australian rhyming slang for 'bottle.' Other examples of Australian rhyming slang include *Joe Blake*, 'a snake,' *jimmygrant*, 'an immigrant,' and *molly the monk*, 'a drunk.'

ascesis the practice of self-discipline. Fittingly enough, it comes from a Greek word meaning 'to exercise.' Many people need to exert their *ascesis* to the utmost in order to force themselves to exercise.

aspectabund an adjective meaning 'having an expressive face.'

aspheterism the belief that there should be no private property; a synonym for *communism*. This word comes from a Greek word meaning 'nothing of one's own.'

asseclist this suggestive combination of letters means 'an attendant or follower' and comes from a Latin word meaning 'to follow after.' But it alludes to so much more that it's a very satisfying word to use.

astrobleme an eroded remnant of a large, ancient crater made by the impact of a meteorite or comet. The term comes from the Greek words for 'star' and 'wound.'

atrabilious an adjective meaning 'melancholy or bad-tempered.' Used mainly in literary writing, it comes from the Latin term *atra bilis,* meaning 'black bile.' In medieval times, black bile was one of the four *cardinal humors,* body fluids whose relative proportions were believed to determine a person's physical and mental qualities. Black bile was thought to cause melancholy: the other three were *yellow bile, phlegm,* and *blood,* associated respectively with irascibility, calmness or stolidity, and optimism.

aucupate a verb meaning 'to go bird-catching.' It also can be used figuratively to mean 'to lie in wait for or hunt.' It comes from Latin words meaning 'bird' and 'catch.'

autochthon a human being born from the soil where he or she lives (like the Biblical Adam). Also used as a synonym for *aborigine,* it comes from a Greek word meaning 'sprung from that land itself.'

autogeneal self-produced, made by yourself. This does not (yet) have a theatrical usage, but it's easy to imagine one: "In his autogeneal play, he explores themes of mania and dissolution." This word comes from a Greek word with the same meaning.

autological of an adjective, having the property that it describes. The antonym is heterological. Thus, the adjective *sesquipedalian* is autological, the adjective *infinitesimal* is heterological.

autophoby the fear of referring to yourself, usually manifested by the reluctance to use the pronouns *I* or *me*. This fear may be based on uncertainty about the proper pronoun to use, or come about through a pathological modesty. Autophobes are fond of using *myself* as a less-frightening replacement for the dread pronouns. "If you have questions, take them up with John or myself." "Alice and myself are going to the movies."

autoptic an adjective meaning 'based on personal observation, eyewitness.' This word is usually used in legal contexts, as in *autoptic testimony* and *autoptic witness*.

autoschediastic done on the spur of the moment or improvised. This word comes from a Greek word meaning 'to act or speak off-hand.' (As luck would have it, this entry itself was put in at the last minute.)

BABLATRICE

...had lunch with Marjorie at the River View – the salad bar alone was worth the trip! There must have been eleven kinds of pasta salad – corkscrews; elbow macaroni; fusilli; penne – plain and the kind with those little grooves down the sides; shells – no, wait a minute, maybe they didn't have shells... NO! I REMEMBER! There WERE shells, they were just more off to the left, and the rest of the pasta salads were on the right. And the BREAD! It was out of this world!!! Pumpernickel, rye, seeded, corn bread...

bablatrice a female babbler. *Chaterestre* is another word for a talkative woman. A *leighster* is a female liar.

balistraria the proper name of those cross-shaped holes in the walls of fortresses and castles, through which weapons (usually crossbows, or *arbalests*) could be fired. Also, a room in which to keep your arbalests. If you're able to fire an arbalest you could be called a *balistrier*.

bandoline a sticky preparation formerly used to set hair in place. From the quotations in the *OED*, it sounds like rather unpleasant stuff: "*the boiled pips* [of quinces] *make the glutinous preparation called* bandoline." The origin of the term is uncertain.

bardolatry a humorous term for excessive admiration of William Shakespeare, who is sometimes referred to as *the Bard* or *the Bard of Avon*. It appears to have been coined by George Bernard Shaw in the early 1900s, together with the related words *bardolater* and *bardolatrous*. *Shakespearolatry* is another word with the same meaning, but this is rarely if ever used.

batie-bummil a useless bungler. An obsolete Scottish dialect word. It is unknown whether there are more useless bunglers in Scotland than elsewhere, or—much more likely—less tolerance of them.

bematist an official road-surveyor in the time of Alexander the Great. This word comes from a Greek word meaning 'to measure by paces.'

bezoar a small hard mass that sometimes forms in the stomachs of certain animals, especially ones that chew the cud, such as goats or sheep. In former times, these lumps were believed to be an antidote for various ailments or conditions: they were either swallowed or rubbed on the affected part of the body. The term comes from a Persian word meaning 'antidote.' A *phytobezoar* is a lump formed chiefly of vegetable matter, while a *trichobezoar* is one formed chiefly of hair.

bibesy an obsolete or perhaps completely invented word from Nathan Bailey's *Universal Etymological Dictionary* of 1731 meaning 'a too earnest desire after drink.' It is taken from a Latin word of Plautus, *bibesia,* meaning 'the land of drinks' or 'the drink-land.'

bicrural two-legged. This word was most likely coined from Latin roots because the non-Latinate word just wasn't jargony or elevated enough. Sadly, although the word *tricrural* exists, no references were found to people running in *tricrural* races. Another fancy *bi-* word, with a citation from 1866, is *biduous,* meaning 'lasting for two days.' *Triduous* is not found, lending more credence to the theory that Victorians did not have three-day weekends.

blaguer a person who talks pretentiously. From a French word, *blague,* meaning 'pretentious falsehood,' self-aggrandizing stories knowing no borders.

blandiose an adjective to describe something that wants to be grand (or has pretensions to grandeur) but is only bland. The word was probably coined by the writer Kenneth Tynan (1927–1980) in the mid-twentieth century.

blastophthoria the hypothetical degeneration of germ cells (sperm cells and egg cells) supposedly caused by alcoholism.

blesiloquent speaking with a lisp or a stammer. From Latin words meaning 'lisping, stammering' and 'speaking.'

BREASTSUMMER

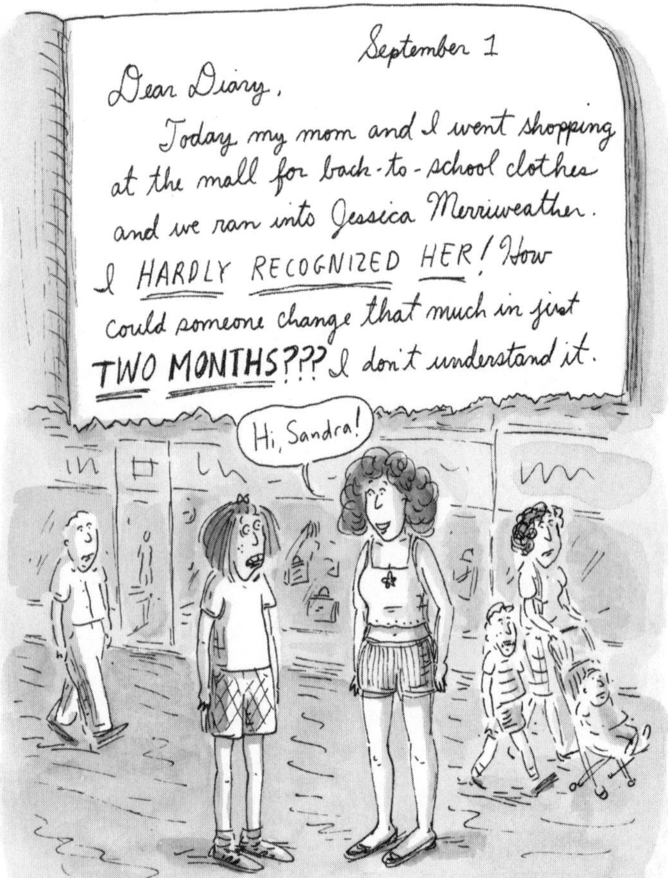

bloviate to speak in a pompous or overbearing way. This is a mock-Latin fancying-up of *blow* or *boast*. The word was made popular by President Warren G. Harding (1865–1923).

breastsummer a large beam, extending horizontally over an opening, that supports the whole weight of the wall above it. The *-summer* part of this word comes from a French word meaning 'beam,' and *breast* is often used, especially in building and nautical compounds, to mean 'support.'

bromatology a treatise on food. A good word for the kind of cookbook that gives you recipes for food that is good for you, instead of for food that you actually want to eat. *Bromo-*, a Greek root meaning 'food,' is also the *bromo-* of *Bromo Seltzer*, and *bromo* on its own (no hyphen) means food that is eaten and not drunk (where does ice cream fit on this continuum?) or a preparation of chocolate. The scientific name of the Cacao plant is *Theobroma cacoa, theobroma* meaning 'food of the gods.'

brume a poetic term meaning 'mist or fog.' It arose in the early nineteenth century and came from a Latin word for 'winter,' as did the adjective *brumous,* meaning 'foggy or wintry.'

cagastrical an adjective used to describe diseases thought to be caused by the influence of malignant stars, which at one time or another included plague and fever. The word comes from Greek roots meaning 'evil star.'

calamistrate a rare verb meaning 'to curl the hair.' This word comes from the Latin word for 'curling-iron.'

callipygian an adjective meaning 'having shapely buttocks.' The term comes from Greek words meaning 'beauty' and 'buttocks'; a related word is *steatopygia,* used to refer to the accumulation of large amounts of fat on the buttocks.

camorra a secret society, usually one breaking the law. This word comes from the name of a group that was active in Naples in the nineteenth century.

campaniform an adjective meaning 'shaped like a bell.' Since such a lot of things are bell-shaped, there are several adjectives with the same meaning, including *campanulous, campanulate,* and *campanular. Campaniliform* means 'shaped like a bell-tower or steeple.'

capnography the measurement of exhaled CO_2, used by anesthesiologists to monitor patients. It comes from a Greek word for 'smoke,' and *-graphy.*

carphology the movements of delirious patients, especially pulling at sheets or blankets, or movements that seem to suggest a search for imaginary objects. This word comes from a Greek word meaning 'collecting straw.'

carriwitchet a pun, a conundrum. The etymology is unknown, making the origin of the word itself a conundrum.

catoptric an adjective meaning 'relating to a mirror or to optical reflection.' This word comes from Greek roots meaning 'against' and 'see.'

catoptromancy divination, i.e., foretelling the future, by means of a mirror. The ending *-mancy* comes from a Greek word meaning 'divination': it is found in many English words for different methods of foretelling the future, for example, *scapulimancy*, divination from the cracks in a burned animal's shoulder blade, *oneiromancy*, divination from dreams, and *chiromancy*, divination from the lines on one's hands.

centessence a nonce-word meaning 'the hundredth essence,' used in contrast to *quintessence*, which literally means 'the fifth essence.' The heavenly bodies were supposed to be made up of quintessence, and the alchemists busied themselves with trying to distill it (when they weren't busy trying to make lead into gold). The *OED* pedantically remarks that the proper word to be the analogue of *quintessence* would be *centesimessence*. We'll get right on that.

chirocracy a very rare word meaning 'government by physical force.'

CLAVUS

choronymy the study of naming, especially place names and names for geographical phenomena, including wind names, hurricane names, and astronomical names. The roots *choro-* and *-nymy* come from the Greek words for 'place' and 'name.'

circumvallate a literary verb meaning 'to surround with a rampart or wall.' The word originated in the seventeenth century as an adjective based on Latin words meaning 'around' and 'rampart.' As an adjective, it does in fact have a special anatomical sense in modern English: it refers to small rounded protuberances, or *papillae,* near the back of the tongue, that are surrounded by taste receptors.

claick the last armful of grain cut at harvest, also called the *kirn-cut, maiden,* or *kirn-baby.* It was often kept and hung by a ribbon above the fireplace.

clavus a pain in the forehead, as though a nail were being driven into it, associated with hysteria. This word comes from a Latin word meaning 'nail.'

clivose an adjective meaning 'hilly, steep.' It comes from the Latin word *clivosus,* which has the same meaning.

cockagrice an unappetizing (to modern palates) dish made of an old cock and a pig boiled and roasted together. *Grice* is an old word for *pig.*

cockyolly bird an expression meaning 'dear little bird,' used both about birds and as an endearment. It is a variant of *dicky-bird.*

codology an Irish word meaning, jocularly, 'the science of leg-pulling.' *Cod* is an Irishism for a joke or a hoax. A hoaxer is called a *codologist.*

colophonian a spurious word, meaning 'relating to a colophon or the conclusion of a book,' originally a mistake for *Colophonian* (with a capital *C*), which means 'an inhabitant of Colophon.' However, the word could still be redeemed—there isn't a word now that means 'relating to a colophon, etc.' (even though there is the word *colophonize,* meaning 'to give a book a colophon'), and this word is as good a candidate as any. *Colophon* (the book word, meaning the inscription at the end of a book that gives facts about its publication, design, etc., or a publisher's emblem on the spine or title page) ultimately comes from a Greek word meaning 'summit, finishing touch.'

comminatory a rare word meaning 'threatening, punitive, or vengeful.' It is related to *commination,* which means 'the threatening of divine vengeance'; both words come from a Latin verb meaning 'to threaten.' In the Anglican liturgy, *commination* refers to the recital of divine threats against sinners that forms part of the service for Ash Wednesday.

contango in the pre-computer age, the fee that a buyer of stock pays to the seller to postpone transfer of the stock to the next or any future settlement date. It was usually paid on a per share or percent basis. The word also has a modern meaning, 'the condition in which distant delivery prices for futures exceed spot prices, often due to the costs of storing and insuring the commodity.' The antonym of *contango* is *backwardation.*

couthy a Scottish word, used to describe a person as 'warm and friendly' or a place as 'cosy and comfortable.' The word arose in the early eighteenth century, apparently from Old English *cuth*, meaning 'known.'

crapulous a literary word meaning 'relating to drunkenness or the drinking of alcohol.' Like the related adjective *crapulent* and noun *crapulence*, it comes from a Latin word meaning 'inebriation,' itself based on a Greek word meaning 'drunken headache.'

cremett another spurious word, this one a mistaken reading of *eremite*, meaning 'inmate of a hospital.' *Eremite* can also mean *hermit*. One can make a nice, completely wrong folk etymology for the mistake by concluding that since people saw hermits so infrequently, of course they couldn't keep the word straight.

criticaster a minor or incompetent critic. The ending *-aster* is used to form nouns referring to someone who is inept or unskillful in a certain sphere of activity, for example, *poetaster*, a person who writes bad poetry, or *medicaster*, a person who falsely claims to have medical skill.

cromulent an adjective meaning 'acceptable; legitimate.' This word comes from an episode of *The Simpsons* in which Bart's teacher, Miss Krabappel, remarks, "Embiggens? I never heard that word before I moved to Springfield." Lisa's teacher, Miss Hoover, replies, "I don't know why. It's a perfectly *cromulent* word." In another episode, Bart makes up the word *kwyjibo*, meaning 'a big, dumb, balding North American ape. With no chin,' which he tries to use in a game of Scrabble with Homer.

cruentation the term for the oozing of blood which occasionally occurs when a cut is made into a dead body. Formerly it was used to mean the supposed bleeding from wounds that would happen when the body of a murdered person was in the presence of the murderer. This comes from a Latin word meaning 'staining with blood.'

deasil an adverb meaning 'clockwise' or 'in the direction of the sun's course,' a direction considered by some to bring luck or good fortune. It comes from a Scottish Gaelic word and is rarely used today; its opposite, *widdershins,* meaning 'anticlockwise' or 'in the opposite direction to the sun's course,' is much less rare.

decemnovenarianize to act like a person of the nineteenth century (a *decemnovenarian*).

decussate having the form of an *X*. This comes from a Latin word meaning 'the number ten' (the Roman numeral for which is, of course, *X*).

deglutition the action of swallowing. The verb, even rarer than the noun, is *deglute*. It could be brought back into fashion with a new figurative sense: "You can't expect me to *deglute* that excuse! What a feat of *deglutition* that would be."

deipnosophist a master of the art of dining. This comes from a Greek word meaning 'one learned in the mysteries of the kitchen.' The plural of this word in Greek was the title of a work by Athenaeus, in which erudite men discuss not only the dishes they were eating but also literary criticism and other miscellaneous topics.

deodand an object that has been the direct cause of the death of a human being (such as a boat from which a person has fallen and drowned) and has been given to the King to be used as an offering to God. This word comes from the Latin for 'that is to be given to God.' This custom was abolished in England in 1846.

diazingiber a kind of ginger candy. *Dia-* is a Greek root meaning 'made of.'

dimidiate to divide into half or reduce by half. Something that is divided in half can be called *dimidiate,* as can a hermaphrodite.

disboscation the clearing of woods to make farmland or pasture. This word isn't used today but could be revived in protests against the clearing of woodland for more shopping malls or housing developments.

disembogue used of a river or stream, this verb means 'to emerge or pour out.' It is found mainly in literary writing and comes from a Spanish word meaning 'to come out of the mouth of a river.'

douzepers a plural noun, being the twelve paladins of Charlemagne, who were the bravest of his knights. The word can also be used to refer to other illustrious knights or nobles.

draffsack a bag of garbage, used figuratively to mean 'a big paunch or belly, a glutton.' *Draff* is an old word meaning 'dregs, swill.'

dragoman an interpreter or professional guide for travelers, especially one in countries in which Arabic, Turkish, or Persian is spoken. It comes from an Arabic word meaning 'interpreter.'

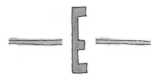

eagre a wave of unusual height, especially a tidal wave up a narrow estuary. The origin remains unknown.

elaqueate to free from a noose or other entanglement. Another literal word that needs a figurative sense: "At first, I felt bad about being laid off, but then I realized I'd been *elaqueated*." A related rare word is *illaqueable,* meaning 'capable of being snared': "I applied there, but I realized the job I wanted wasn't *illaqueable*."

emacity a fondness for buying things. The word comes from a Latin verb meaning 'to buy': it has always been extremely rare and, despite the increasing materialism of recent decades, shows no sign of becoming any less so!

empasm a perfumed powder sprinkled on the body to prevent sweating or for medicinal purposes. A similar word with the same meaning is *diapasm*: both come from a Greek verb meaning 'to sprinkle.' There is no recorded use of either word since the late nineteenth century.

emunctory relating to the blowing of the nose. *Emunction* is 'the action of wiping the nose.' Both these words come from Latin words with the same meanings. The rare word *emunct,* meaning 'of keen or acute judgment,' comes from a Latin phrase that means 'a man of keen scent' or 'a man with a wiped nose.'

emydosaurian a crocodile. This fancy term comes from the roots *emyd-,* meaning 'turtle,' and *-saurian,* meaning 'lizard.'

entortillation the action of entwining or twisting. This comes from a Latin word meaning 'to twist.'

erethism painful, unhealthy overexcitement, especially of the mental powers or passions. This comes from a Greek word meaning 'to irritate,' and a misspelling, *erythism*, appeared in quite a few medical books.

ergophobic someone who fears work. Usually, this word is used jocularly.

erinaceous an adjective meaning 'like a hedgehog.' It is mostly used in a zoological sense but cries out for a figurative use to describe people with prickly or bristly manners.

erubescent a rare adjective meaning 'reddening or blushing.' It is based on a Latin verb meaning 'to be red': a related word in English is *rubicund*, an adjective which refers to a ruddy or high-colored facial complexion.

esemplastic an adjective meaning 'molding into one' or 'unifying.' Coined by Samuel Taylor Coleridge (1772–1834) in the early nineteenth century to refer to the power of the human imagination, it was probably suggested by a German word with the same meaning, *Ineinsbildung*. There are very few recorded examples of its use outside Coleridge's own writings.

eutrapely a sadly obsolete word for 'pleasantness in conversation,' one of the seven moral virtues enumerated by Aristotle. In the New Testament, it was used to mean 'a reprehensible levity of speech.'

exauctorate to depose or oust from office, to deprive of authority. This comes from a Latin word meaning 'to dismiss from service.'

exonym a name that foreigners use for a place (instead of the name that people who live there use), such as *Cologne* for *Köln* and *Florence* for *Firenze*.

expergefaction waking up, from a Latin word meaning 'make awake.' Alarm clocks could be called *expergefactors*.

FESTUCEOUS

faitour a cheat, especially a person who shams illness or tells fortunes; an impostor. Since there never seem to be enough derogatory terms to apply to all those who deserve them, this word may come in handy.

fankle a Scottish word meaning 'to tangle or entangle something.' It comes from Scots *fank*, which means 'a coil of rope.'

festuceous an obsolete and rare word meaning 'like a straw.' A related word is *festucaceous*, which means 'like a stalk.' They both come from a Latin root meaning 'stalk.'

feuillemorte an adjective meaning 'having the color of a dead or faded leaf' (i.e., brown or yellowish brown). It comes from the French for 'dead leaf.' Other, less Frenchy forms are *filemot, philemort,* and *phillimot.*

flagitation the action of asking or demanding with passion; begging. A useful word for parents everywhere: "If you don't stop that *flagitation* right now, my answer will be no!"

fleer to laugh in a disrespectful or jeering way. A rare word found mainly in literary writing, it is probably of Scandinavian origin and is related to a Norwegian and Swedish dialect verb meaning 'to grin.'

flexanimous an adjective meaning 'having the power to influence, moving, affecting.' It comes from Latin words meaning 'bend' and 'mind.'

florisugent an adjective meaning 'sucking honey from flowers,' used for birds and insects. It comes from Latin words meaning 'flower' and 'suck.'

forbysen an obsolete word meaning 'an example, a parable, a proverb, or a token.' *Bysen,* by itself, can also mean 'a shocking thing.'

foudroyant an adjective meaning 'thundering, noisy.' This word comes from a French word meaning 'to strike with lightning.'

freck an obsolete Scottish word meaning 'to move quickly or nimbly.' *To make freck* is 'to make ready,' and *freck* can also mean 'keen for mischief, ready for trouble.' The word may come from an older word meaning 'greedy' or 'courageous.'

fremescence a rare word meaning 'an incipient roaring.' Another word useful for parents, who can swoop in with a toy or other distraction when they see an infant's *fremescence.*

fuliginous an adjective meaning 'sooty or dusky.' Found chiefly in the literature of the past, it comes from the Latin word for 'soot.'

funambulist a tightrope walker. *Funambulists funambule,* if a verb is needed. These words come from the Latin words of the same meaning (it seems as though *funambuling* is a staple of western civilization). The word can also be used figuratively to describe people who think quickly on their feet.

funestation an adjective meaning 'pollution from touching a dead body.' The word *funest* means 'causing death or evil, disastrous.' Both words are related to *funeral*.

fylfot (or *fylfot cross*) another name for the design called a *cross cramponnee, gammadion,* or *swastika.*

FREAKISH AND FANTASTIC FORNICATIONS

Given the amount of time

that people through the ages have spent either in the activity or contemplating it (if such thinking can, in fact, be called contemplation), it's not surprising that there are so many varied words defined stodgily as 'fornication.' There's the fairly ancient *forlie*, usually used with *by* or *with*, in phrases like "and with him to be *forlayne*." Coming later are other *fornicarious* words   the more entertaining *houghmagandy* (Scots, of course), *fellowred, patha patha, scortation,* and *holoury*. If you participate in such behavior, you should be prepared to hear the *lenonian* ('belonging to a bawd') terms *apple-squire, bismer, belswagger, holard, horel, horeling, limb-lifter, mackerel, molrower, mutton-monger, putour, putrer, sheep-biter, smockster, striker* (or *stringer*), or *tweak* muttered in your direction. You might also be called a *fornicarer*, which sounds like a more emotionally involved fornicator (but isn't). If accused of *bordel* or *palliardry,* you might have to pay a *lairwite* 'a fine for fornication or adultery, especially with a bondwoman.' You might "be *meynt* in joyfulnesse," of course, or have *ymone* (or *mone* or *mene*), or go *a-mollocking* (a word coined by Stella Gibbons in the hilarious *Cold Comfort Farm*). Only women are accused of *bitchery, drabbery, putery,* or *strumpery,* as much as the other sex may participate or benefit therefrom. There's *subagitate* (depending upon the circumstances, of course), which has nothing to do with what we now think of as agitation, and even less to do with submarines. *Wifthing*, an obsolete word (from *wife* + *thing*, believe it or not), can mean 'sexual intercourse'; more romantically, it can also mean 'wedding.' If your partnership is not exclusive, or your cohabitation only temporary, you can describe it as *syndyasmian* (from a Greek word meaning 'to couple.')

There must be a twelve-step group for whoremongerers somewhere.

If the more ordinary expressions of love are not your style, you may have to resort to more unusual words. You may have *algolagnia*, and be both masochistic and sadistic. Or you might have *kleptolagnia*, and only be aroused by theft, or *iconolagnia*, like Pygmalion, and only be moved by an image of your own making. *Urolagnia* is arousal from urination, but is fairly rare. You might be invited to a *partouse*, slang for 'orgy,' or read *fladge*, pornographic literature concentrating on flagellation. And although *pornerastic* sounds like a modern word, it was used in 1870 and means 'addicted to whoremongering.' There must be a twelve-step group for whoremongerers somewhere.

A rare but helpful adjective that can describe all the words above is *syngamical*, 'pertaining to copulation.' If not a word of this entertained you, perhaps you are *anaphroditous*, 'without sexual desire.'

gaberlunzie an old Scottish word for a beggar, found frequently in Scottish literature of the early nineteenth century. It was also used to refer to a *beadsman*, who was someone paid to pray for the soul of another person. The origin of the word is unknown.

gallinipper a large mosquito. The etymology is unclear but the word is mainly used in the United States.

gammerstang a tall, awkward woman. Related words are *gomerel*, 'fool, simpleton,' and *gamphrel*, 'blockhead.' Without the 'awkward' part, such a person could be described as *leptosomatic*, 'lean and tall.'

glaistig a Gaelic word for a beautiful fairy, usually seen at the bank of a stream. Also, a hag in the shape of a goat.

gongoozler a person who stares at activity on a canal. This highly specific word has since been broadened to mean any kind of idler or rubbernecker.

grandgore syphilis. Another word that sounds much nicer than what it actually means.

gricer a train-spotter, someone who braves rainy and windy station platforms to catch a glimpse of unusual trains. An unproved etymology holds that this word comes from a humorous pronunciation of *grouse*, making the connection between the supposed resemblance of train-spotting to grouse-shooting. The verb *grice* and the noun *gricing* are back-formations from *gricer*.

gulosity a rare word meaning 'gluttony, greediness, voracity.' *Gulous* is another rare word with the same meaning, from the same Latin root *gula-*.

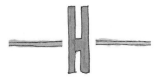

hagioscope an opening cut in the wall of a church to let worshippers in a side aisle or chapel see the elevation of the host during the service. This is also called, less graciously, a *squint*.

halch to hug or embrace. One citation for this word in the *OED*'s files, from about 1650, seems to have been used self-consciously to sound classically old-fashioned, even then.

hebetude a literary word meaning 'dullness or lethargy.' It comes from a Latin adjective meaning 'blunt.'

heisenbug an error in a computer program that disappears or behaves differently when you attempt to fix or isolate it. Computing jargon, this word comes from Werner Heisenberg's Uncertainty Principle in quantum physics, the principle that the momentum and position of a particle cannot both be known precisely at the same time—the attempt to determine one makes it impossible to know the other.

hemianopsia half-blindness, or loss of perception of one-half of the field of vision. Only used in the specialist sense to date, but crying out for a figurative use: "Whenever his parents fight his *hemianopsia* kicks in, and he's only able to see his father's side of the argument."

herisson a structure like a wooden horse covered with spikes or points, used as a military punishment. The person being punished was made to ride it. It comes from a Latin word meaning 'hedgehog.'

hierodule a slave who lives in a temple and is dedicated to the service of a god. *Heiro-* is a Greek root meaning 'holy' and shows up in a great many words, such as *hieromonarch*, 'a monk who is also a priest,' *hieromnemnon*, 'a sacred recorder,' *hierography*, 'the description of religions,' and *hierophobia*, 'fear of sacred things.'

hippotomist an accomplished horse-dissector. *Hippo-* is the Greek root meaning 'horse,' and *-tomy* is a Greek root meaning 'cut.'

hodmandod any strange person, a scarecrow. This word has the equally wonderful variants *hodmadod, hodmedod, hodman Hob,* and *hodmandon.*

hoghenhine a member of one's family. It comes from *oen hine*, Middle English for 'own hind,' and was chiefly used in legal contexts. *Hind* is an old word for 'servant.'

hogo a stink. This comes from an anglicized spelling of the French *haut goût,* meaning 'high savor or flavor.'

honeyfuggle to swindle, cheat. This word is American slang and apparently from *honey* plus *fugle,* meaning 'to cheat, trick.'

hongi a traditional Maori greeting or salutation made by pressing or touching noses.

houghmagandy sexual intercourse with a person one is not married to. A rare word, it is found mainly in Scottish writing of the eighteenth and early nineteenth centuries, though it also appears in Vladimir Nabokov's *Pale Fire* (1962): "She would have preferred him to have gone through a bit of wholesome *houghmagandy* with the wench."

ICONOMACH

ichthyarchy the domain of the fishes, the fish-world. A nonce-word used in 1853, but lovely in its ornate simplicity.

iconomach a rare word meaning 'one who is hostile to images.'

idolothyous an adjective meaning 'sacrificed to an idol.' The noun is *idolothyte*, and the word *idolothytic* means 'characterized by the eating of meat sacrificed to idols.' Waste not, want not.

igarape in South America, a stream wide enough for a canoe.

ignicolist a fire-worshipper. *Ignivomous* is another uncommon word with the *igni-* 'fire' root; it means 'vomiting fire.' Perhaps a happy occasion if one worships fire, but otherwise not. *Ignivomous*, unsurprisingly, is mostly used literally about volcanoes and figuratively about foul-mouthed people.

ikbal a member of the harem of an Ottoman sultan, especially a favorite of the Sultan.

illatration an act of barking at someone or something. This word is used figuratively but would be useful to make distinctions between dogs barking just to bark, and dogs barking at a particular thing or person (e.g., a car, a burglar, a mail carrier).

IRREGULAR AND INCREDIBLE ILLNESSES

Many words for diseases

are certainly weird, but it takes a morbid turn of mind to find them wonderful. It's not clear where to lay the blame for the weirdness of medical words. Difficult Greek and Latin roots are always good suspects, as is the natural desire of the healer to obfuscate, so as to seem to be the holder of arcane knowledge (and thus the only one with a cure). And, as is often the case, when the words are weird, what they mean is even weirder. Who would want to suffer from *alastrim* 'a contagious disease that resembles smallpox'? (Even the slightest resemblance to smallpox is too much of one.) Or *ascarias* 'infestation of the gastrointestinal canal'? (The citation for this one in the *OED* is a particular horror: "An epidemic of *ascariasis* on a skunk-farm." [1923 *Nature* 19 May]) "You've got *bagassosis*" sounds like a schoolyard taunt, but it has nothing to do with too-big trousers. It's a disease of the lungs from inhaling the dust of sugar cane waste. While you're worrying about your lungs you can ponder *byssinosis*—a chronic disease of the lungs caused by inhalation of fine textile particles, especially cotton dust, over a long period. How long have you been inhaling cotton dust, anyway? (Ever since you first pulled a T-shirt over your head, probably.)

At this point you may want to initiate *decumbiture*—the act of going to bed when sick. (This word is formed irregularly from Latin. If it had been formed "correctly" it would be *decubiture*. Perhaps the coiner was too ill to care.) The word is also used to denote an astrological reading taken for the time you took to your bed, in order to determine (by consulting the stars and planets) if you will live or die.

Perhaps your disorder is not purely physical. If, when set on your feet, you begin to leap, you may have *saltatoric spasms*. You may repeat the same word or phrase in a meaningless fashion, or *verbigerate*. If you have ever lived in Siberia, or certain non-European countries, you may have *miryachit,* a disease in which the sufferer mimics everything said or done by another. Like nearly everyone else, you might have *fever-lurden* 'the disease of laziness.'

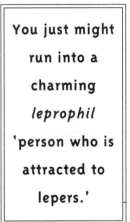

You just might run into a charming *leprophil* 'person who is attracted to lepers.'

Sometimes the cure is worse than the disease. You might seek *dipsopathy* 'the treatment of disease by abstaining from liquids.' This word comes from Greek words meaning 'thirst' and 'suffering' and was modeled on the words *homeopathy* and *hydropathy*. As might be expected, neither the cure nor the word ever really caught on. If that doesn't sound soothing, you could go in for *glossoscopy* 'the inspection or observation of the tongue for the purposes of diagnosis.' That is, if you can find a competent *glossologist*. Do you still feel *meseling* 'leprous'? Don't worry, you just might run into a charming *leprophil* 'person who is attracted to lepers.'

Did reading this *nosology* 'list or catalogue of known diseases' make you ill? Here's wishing you a quick return to *invalescence* 'strength, health.'

illeism excessive reference to oneself in the third person; especially excessive use of the pronoun *he.*

illywhacker an informal Australian word meaning 'a small-time confidence trickster.' It can be traced back to the 1940s, but its origin is unknown.

imborsation an Italian method of electing magistrates in which the names of the candidates are put in a bag and the winners are drawn out. The lone citation from the *OED* has eight hundred names being put in the purse but no mention of the number of magistrate-winners.

immensikoff a slang term for a heavy overcoat trimmed with fur, supposedly from "The Shoreditch Toff," a popular song from about 1868, in which there are the lines "I fancy I'm a toff, From top to toe I really think I looks—*Immensikoff.*" (A *toff* is a stylish man.) The singer of the song, Arthur Lloyd, wore such an overcoat.

impignorate to pawn or mortgage something. This comes from a Latin word meaning 'to pledge.' To *repignorate* is to redeem a pledge.

indagatrix an obsolete and rare word meaning 'a female searcher or investigator.' It is the feminine of the Latin word *indagator,* meaning 'a tracer, an investigator.'

inhume a poetic verb meaning 'to bury someone or something.' The word for the reverse process, *exhume,* is rather more familiar in current English: both come from a Latin word for 'ground.'

inunct a very rare word meaning 'to apply ointment to someone or something.'

iotacist someone who makes excessive use of the letter *i*. Originally meaning the changing of the pronunciation of other Greek vowels to be more like the pronunciation of the vowel *iota*, this word could have a new use as a way to refer to someone boastful and self-centered.

ithyphallic an adjective meaning 'indecent, obscene,' from association with its other meaning, 'having an erect phallus.' It comes from the practice of carrying a phallus (a model, one hopes) in procession at festivals of Bacchus. The *ithy-* part comes from a Greek word meaning 'straight.' The implication that curved phalli were also used is not borne out by the etymological record, as there is no word in the *OED* meaning 'curved phallus.'

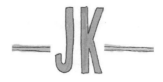

jiffle to fidget or shuffle. This is just one of several words that can mean 'fidget' and end in -*le*, including *figgle, fissle, nestle, sessle, tiddle,* and *trifle.*

jumentous a very rare adjective meaning 'resembling horse's urine.' In the nineteenth century, the Sydenham Society's *Lexicon of Medicine and Allied Sciences* defined this word as 'a term applied to urine which is high colored, strong smelling, and turbid, like that of the horse.' It comes from *jument,* an obsolete word that means 'a beast of burden.'

karoshi death caused by overwork or job-related exhaustion. A Japanese term, it came into general use in the late 1980s, although it is still used only in the context of workers in Japan. It derives from words meaning 'excess,' 'labor,' and 'death.'

katsuramono one of the types of Japanese Noh drama, in which the chief character is female and the theme romantic. It is usually presented as the third play in a performance of Noh. A man who plays female roles in Kabuki drama is known as an *onnagata* or *oyama.*

kenspeckle a Scottish word meaning 'conspicuous, easily recognizable.' The origin is not precisely known, but it may be related to a Swedish word meaning 'quick at recognizing people or things.'

kinnikinnick a substance consisting of dried sumac leaves and willow or dogwood bark, smoked by North American Indians as a tobacco substitute or mixed together with tobacco. The word comes from Unami, an extinct Algonquian language, in which its meaning was 'mixture.'

kurdaitcha an Australian word for a malignant supernatural being, taken from the word for the shoes worn to ward off such a creature. The shoes were made of the feathers of an emu stuck together with human blood.

lacustrine an adjective meaning 'associated with lakes.' Taken from the Latin word for lake, it is used chiefly in technical contexts, as in *lacustrine sediments* or *lacustrine fish*.

langsuir a female vampire that preys on newborn children. The *langsuir* (a Malayan monster) wears a green robe, has long black hair that covers the hole on the back of her neck (through which she sucks the blood of children), emits a whinnying cry, and can take the shape of an owl. All in all, a terrifying creature. Another Malay vampire is the *penanggalan*, which also preys on newborns but has the form of a human head with a stomach sac attached.

lerky a children's game in which all the players but one hide and a tin can is placed in a ring. The players then try to kick the can out of the ring without being seen.

limerance the initial exhilarating rush of falling in love; the state of being in love. This word was coined by Dorothy Tennov in a 1979 book titled *Love and Limerance*. Psychologists have found that this state lasts for an average of three years.

limicolous living in mud. Usually applied to birds or worms, this word comes from Latin words meaning 'mud' and 'to inhabit.' A related adjective is *limicoline*. Something that lives in the open part of a freshwater lake or pond, not near the muddy edges or bottom, is *limnetic*, from a Greek word meaning 'living in marshes.'

liripoop the tail of a graduate's hood (an archaic feature of academic dress). The *liripoop* (etymology unknown) hung down the back when the hood was off, and it was wrapped like a bandage around the head when the hood was on. Like most academic dress, the *liripoop* is both intimidating to others and uncomfortable for the wearer.

logodaedaly ingenious or cunning use of words. *Logo-* comes from a Greek root meaning 'word,' and *-daedaly* is related to *Daedalus*, the name of the designer of the Labyrinth for the Minotaur of Crete. His name has come to mean 'ingenious, skillful.' Another rare *logo-* word is the nonce-word *logopandocie*, which is the 'readiness to admit words of all kinds' and describes the English language (and most lexicographers).

longicorn a kind of beetle with very long antennae. The word comes from Latin words meaning 'long' and 'horn,' and it is a good example of a word with a perfectly serviceable etymology that still sounds made-up.

longinquity a rare word meaning 'long distance, remoteness.' From a Latin word meaning 'long, distant.'

loon-slatt an obsolete slang name for an old Scottish coin worth thirteen pence halfpenny, the proverbial amount of the hangman's fee.

lubitorium a service station. This word apparently comes from *lubricate* plus the suffix *–torium* (as in *auditorium*).

luer a mechanical connection and seal used in medical machinery, especially IVs and other devices needing air- or watertight seals. It's pronounced "LOOer."

luscition poor eyesight. This comes from a Latin word meaning 'one-eyed.'

lushburg a counterfeit coin, made to look like an English silver penny, imported from Luxembourg during the reign of Edward III. *Lushberg* is an anglicization of *Luxembourg*.

lyssophobia a fear of rabies so extreme that the sufferer actually manifests symptoms of the disease. This word comes from a Greek word meaning 'rabies' and the suffix *-phobia*.

LEARNED AND LAUDABLE -LOGIES

The suffix -*logy*, from a Greek word

meaning 'discourse, speak,' has been applied to form the names of all manner of sciences, both practical and absurd.

There's *balneology*, the medical study of bathing, and *escapology*, the study of the methods and technique of escaping. *Garbology*, the study of garbage as a social science, is probably more than tangentially related to *loimology*, the study of pestilential diseases. Someone who studies giants is interested in *gigantology*; and the study of mummies is *momiology*. The study of giant mummies, if there is such a thing, could be *gigantomomiology*. *Ptochology* is the study of unemployment and poverty (unfortunately a very rich field) and *squalorology* is the study of squalor. Once you're done with squalor (although a fascinating subject) you could move on to *acology*, the study of the methods of curing disease. Or to *anatripsology*, the study of the uses of friction. Or further still to *barology*, the study of weight, or *cyesiology*, the study of pregnancy, or *emmenology*, the study of menstruation. The study of hypnotism is *neurypnology*. The study of the sense of smell is *osphresiology*.

The study of the history of existing animals is *cainozoology*, as opposed to the investigation of the history of extinct animals, which is *paleozoology*. The study of imaginary animals would be, possibly, *phantastizoology*, but that word itself is imaginary. The study of fossil footprints is *ichnology*. The study of apparently useless rudimentary organs of plants and animals is *dysteleology*.

Of course, you could just throw in the towel on all the other -*logies* and devote yourself solely to *agnoiology*, the investigation into the character and conditions of ignorance. Or you could study *oudenology*, the science of things having no real existence (from a Greek root meaning 'nothing' and -*ology*). It might just be your lot to dabble in *deontology*, the science of duty and moral obligation, or *hamartiology*, the study of sin, or *ponerology*, the science of evil, or *heortology*, the study of the feasts of the Christian year. You could also engage in *naology*, the study of sacred buildings.

The study of giant mummies, if there is such a thing, could be *gigantomomiology*.

The study of slugs is *limacology*. (The *lima bean* is not related, being named for the capital of Peru.) The study of cooking is *magirology*. The study of entrails is *splanchnology*, which sounds onomatopoeic but is not. The science of spirit-rapping (as in seances) is *typtology*. The science of joining (as in rivets, not in social clubs) is *zygology*.

There are many -*logies* that begin with *P*. The study of the origin of personal names is *patronomatology*. The science of counter-espionage is *phylactology*. The study of rivers is *potamology*. The scientific study of the face is *prosopology*. The study of the art of artillery is *pyroballogy*.

If none of these sciences interest you, you could begin your study of *pantology*, the systematic view of all branches of knowledge. Good luck!

macilent an adjective meaning both 'thin' (as in weight) and 'lacking in substance' (as in worth), ideal for giving ambiguous compliments.

mackabroin an obsolete and rare word meaning 'an old hag.' It comes from *macabre,* whose origin is obscure. The word did come from French, but whether the French word came from *Maccabeus* (as in Judas Maccabeus) or from another name is not known.

macushla an affectionate form of address, used in Irish English. It comes from the Irish words *mo,* meaning 'my,' and *cuisle,* 'pulse'; a similar Irish word is *acushla,* from the phrase *a chuisle (moi chroi),* 'O pulse (of my heart)!'

mammothrept a spoiled child. This wonderful word comes from a Greek word meaning 'raised by one's grandmother.'

marcescible an adjective meaning 'tending or likely to wither or fade.' From a Latin word meaning 'to be faint.'

marrowsky a kind of slang or error in speaking in which there is a transposition of the first letters, syllables, or parts of two words. Supposedly this comes from the name of the Polish count Joseph Boruwlaski (1739–1837), who was a famous dwarf living in Britain.

materteral an adjective meaning 'like an aunt.' Usually used humorously, it comes from a Latin word meaning 'maternal aunt.' (Maternal in the sense of being related through one's mother, not in the sense of 'motherly feeling,' although that is what is implied by the word *materteral.*)

matranee in India, a female servant who has to do all the nastiest work. One can hear thousands of Indian mothers saying to ungrateful offspring, "What do you think I am, your *matranee?*"

meacock a coward or effeminate person. The word is rarely found after the eighteenth century, although the *OED* does have one example of its use in 1921, from *Ulysses* by James Joyce. Its origin is unknown.

meliturgy honey-making or bee-keeping. From a Greek word meaning 'bee-keeping.'

milce-witter an adjective meaning 'knowing mercy.' A similar adjective is *milce-hearted.*

milliad a thousand years. Formed (the *OED* says 'badly') from *mille,* Latin for 'one thousand,' on the example of *myriad.*

monarsenous this word does not mean, as one might think, 'having only one arse'; instead it means 'having only one male for several females.' Used mostly in zoological contexts, it seems apt for unbalanced dinner parties or junior-high dances. (In which case, perhaps the 'arse' interpretation could be revived, depending on the behavior of the male attendees.)

monkey's wedding simultaneous rain and sunshine. This informal South African term probably comes from a Portuguese expression translated as 'vixen's wedding,' which has the same meaning, but there is also a possibility that it entered South African English from a Zulu phrase.

mournival a set of four kings, queens, jacks, or aces in one hand, or any set of four things or people. This comes from a French word whose literal meaning is 'a slap in the face.'

mouton enragé literally, 'mad sheep.' A term for an angry person who is usually calm.

mucronate an adjective meaning 'coming to a hard sharp point.' The pencils of the truly detail-oriented can be described as *mucronate*.

muliebrity womanly qualities or womanliness. The term comes from the Latin word for woman: unlike its masculine counterpart *virility* (from the Latin for 'man'), it is rarely used except in formal or literary writing.

mundation the action of cleaning or the state of being clean. From a Latin word meaning 'clean.'

mundungus a rare word meaning 'bad-smelling tobacco.' It comes from a humorous use of a Spanish word meaning 'tripe.'

mussitation muttering, murmuring. From a Latin word with the same meaning.

mututatial a rare word meaning 'something borrowed.'

neoteny the preservation of juvenile characteristics well into maturity, especially where these characteristics are attractive. This word comes from Greek roots meaning 'extend' and 'young.'

nexility speed or pithiness of speech. (This entry deliberately left short as an example.)

nidgery an obsolete adjective meaning 'trifling, fidgety, foppish.' It comes from a (now also obsolete) French word meaning the same thing.

nidor the smell of burning fat, or any strong meat-cooking smell. It has been applied, unfortunately, to the smell of burning martyred flesh: "The *nidor* of a human creature roasted for faith."

niefling a nongendered word meaning 'a niece or nephew,' useful as shorthand, e.g., "I promised my sister that I'd watch my *nieflings* this Saturday." This word was coined by Susan Parker Martin of New York.

nighwhat an obsolete adverb meaning 'nearly, almost.' Perhaps because it's obsolete, it sounds very hillbillyish to modern ears: "He was *nighwhat* kilt when that there hog jumped onto his truck!"

nihilarian a person who deals with things of no importance (whether by choice or not is unclear). Formed from the Latin root *nihil-*, meaning 'nothing,' on the example of *unitarian*, etc.

nim a game in which two players take one or more counters from any one of several piles, the goal being to force one's opponent to take the last counter (or sometimes, to take it oneself). This word may come either from another *nim*, meaning 'thief,' or perhaps from the German word *nehmen*, meaning 'to take.'

nimfadoro an effeminate fellow, especially one who is well-dressed and popular with women. The example in the *OED*, a quote from the playwright Ben Jonson, talks about the *nimfadoro* wearing 'white virgin boot[s].'

ninguid an adjective meaning 'having much snow,' used to describe a place. From a Latin word *ninguis*, meaning 'snow.'

nippitate an obscure word meaning 'good strong ale.' The word is sometimes found with faux-Latin endings, such as *nippitatum* and *nippitati*.

nithing an archaic word for a contemptible or despicable person. It arose at the beginning of the eleventh century from Old Norse, and it later developed the additional meaning of 'a mean or miserly person.'

niveous an adjective meaning 'snowy' or 'resembling snow.' A word used mainly in literary writing, it comes from the Latin word for snow.

nomothete a rare word meaning 'a lawgiver or legislator.' *Nomo-* is a Greek word meaning 'law.' Other *nomo-* words include *nomography,* 'the expression of law in written form,' *nomology,* 'the inductive science of law' or 'the science of the conformity of action to rules,' and *nomocracy,* 'government based on a legal code.'

nundination buying and selling, trade. From the Latin word *nundine,* a market-day held every eight (by Roman counting, nine) days.

nychthemeral an adjective that means 'occurring with a variation that matches night and day.' It comes from a Greek word meaning 'lasting for a day and a night.' A *nychthemeron* is a period of twenty-four hours. These words are fairly rare, but one can imagine their use quite easily: "'Not one *nychthemeron* more shall I tarry,' cried the heroine," or "They complained about the *nychthemeral* variation in traffic outside of the Hamptons' hottest nightspot."

nyctophobia extreme or irrational fear of the night or of darkness. It comes from the Greek word for night: a related word in English is *nyctalopia,* the term for a medical condition characterized by the inability to see at night or in dim light.

obliquangled an obsolete form (but wonderful to say) of *oblique-angled*. A good figurative use would be to extend this word to mean 'messy, awkward': "I tried to put it together but it got all *obliquangled*."

ochlophobia extreme or irrational fear of or aversion to crowds. A very rare term, it comes from a Greek word meaning 'crowd' or 'mob.'

octothorpe the telephone keypad symbol '#'; also called *pound, number sign, hash,* or *crosshatch*. This key and the '*' *(asterisk)* key were introduced by Bell Laboratories in the early 1960s on the then-new touch-tone telephones. Don MacPherson, a Bell Labs engineer, coined the word from *octo-* (for the eight points) and *Thorpe* (Mr. MacPherson was active in an organization lobbying for the return of Jim Thorpe's Olympic medals. His medals were taken away after it was revealed that he was not strictly an amateur, having been paid for playing baseball when he was a youth. The medals were posthumously restored in 1982).

oggannition an obsolete and rare word meaning 'snarling, growling.' From a Latin word meaning 'yelp or growl at.'

oligosyllable a word of fewer than four syllables. *Oligo-* comes from a Greek root meaning 'small, little, few.'

omophagy the eating of raw food, especially raw meat. The word was originally used in reference to feasts for the Greek god Bacchus, at which raw flesh was eaten. It comes from the Greek for 'raw.'

ONOLATRY

omphaloskeptic a person who indulges in navel-gazing; that is, someone who is self-absorbed. Unless, of course, one means the *omphalopsychites*, who engaged in navel-gazing as a means of bringing on a hypnotic reverie. *Omphalo-* comes from a Greek word meaning 'navel.' Another fun *omphalo-* word is *omphalomancy*, which is the practice of predicting the number of future children of a mother by counting the knots in the first child's umbilical cord.

onolatry a very rare word meaning 'the worship of donkeys or asses.' It is taken from a Greek word meaning 'ass,' and another word based on this root is *onocentaur*, a term from Greek mythology that refers to a centaur with the body of an ass rather than that of a horse.

ooglification the substitution of an "OO" sound for another vowel sound to make a standard English word into a slang word or to make a slang word even slangier. *Cigaroot* for *cigarette* is a good example of *ooglification*. We may not be seeing *phoot* for *phat* any time soon, though.

opsimath a person who begins to learn or study late in life. A rare term, it comes from Greek words meaning 'late' and 'to learn.' A related word in English is *polymath*, a person with a very wide range of knowledge.

orcost poverty, indigence. This word comes from an Old Norse word meaning 'want.'

oredelf the right to dig minerals; the digging of ore. An obsolete legal term, this comes from *ore* plus the word *delf*, meaning 'mine, digging.' *Delf* is related to *ditch*.

orgulous an adjective meaning 'proud' or 'haughty,' found chiefly in very literary writing. It dates from Middle English, and there is almost no evidence of its use after the sixteenth century until the writers Robert Southey (1774–1843) and Walter Scott (1771–1832) began to employ it as a historical archaism in the early 1800s.

ostrobogulous a word meaning 'bizarre, unusual, or interesting.' This word is associated with the writer Victor B. Neuberg (1883–1940), who gave it the etymology 'full of (from Latin *ulus*) rich (from Greek *ostro*) dirt (schoolboy *bog*).' Related words include *ostrobogulatory, ostrobogulation,* and *ostrobogulosity.*

otacust an obsolete word meaning 'eavesdropper, spy.' From Greek roots meaning 'ear' and 'listener.'

oxter a Scottish and northern English word for a person's armpit. It comes from Old English.

palang the practice, originating in Borneo, of piercing the penis with a gold or tin bolt. In the middle of the bolt is a hole to allow for urination. This practice is said to have persisted in Borneo until at least 1974, and it is occasionally done in the United States today as elective body modification.

palestral an adjective meaning 'pertaining to wrestling' (and by extension, to athletics in general). From a Greek word meaning 'to wrestle.'

pampination the trimming of vines. From a Latin word meaning 'vine-shoot.'

pandiculation the stretching of the body that often accompanies yawning. This word is also sometimes used to mean yawning itself. It comes from a Latin word meaning 'to stretch oneself.'

panmixis a population in which random mating takes place. Mostly applied to animals but equally well-suited to any large city or college campus.

pannage the right to pasture pigs in a wood, or the payment for that right. This might be useful to revive as a modern word for dog-walking privileges in a yard or common area, and it might encourage pet owners to apply for (and pay for) such rights.

panthnetist someone who believes that both the body and soul perish in death. From Greek roots meaning 'all' and 'mortal.'

parergon secondary work or business, separate from one's main work or ordinary employment. A handy (and cloaking) synonym for *moonlighting*. From Greek roots meaning 'beside' and 'work.'

pareschatology the name given to the study of theories about life after physical death but before the final (Christian) resurrection. The word comes from a Greek word meaning 'study of next to last things' (the last thing being resurrection). *Eschatology* is the study of last things.

pasquinade a satirical piece of writing posted in a public place. *Pasquin* was the name of a statue in Rome that was often dressed up to resemble a mythological or historical figure on St. Mark's Day (April 25th). Students often composed verses to salute Pasquin on his big day, and the verses were written on or posted by the statue. The verses soon became satirical and the custom spread to other countries, where satirical writings (with or without the benefit of convenient statues to rest upon) were often signed "Pasquin."

passiuncle a petty or contemptible passion. This is a nonce-word that deserves a wider field. "He has a *passiuncle* for Ring Dings." Formed from the word *passion* with the diminutive ending -*uncle*, on the example of *vibratiuncle*, 'a slight vibration.'

pedinomite a person who lives on a plain. From a Greek word meaning 'plain-dweller.'

pedotrophy the bringing up or raising of children. The British spelling is *paedotrophy*. A particularly good mother or father could be described as a *pedotrophist*. However, given the general tenor and the recent trends in memoir, if this word finds a new popularity, it is sure to be in the negative: "My parents were by no means *pedotrophists*..."

PECULIAR AND PRODIGIOUS PIGS

Although theology and science

seem to have more than their fair share of weird words, the most mundane things can often be described by unusual words. The *gussie* or *grunting-cheat* ('pig') is quite possibly the most mundane of animals, but is described by many fascinating *suillary* ('of swine') or *aprine* ('of wild swine') terms.

The pig's snout, that icon of piggishness, is a *rowel*. With it, a pig can *whick* or *wrine* 'squeal', or *grout* 'turn up the ground.' Of course, a pig can also *moil* 'wallow' in the mud.

A pig-sty is a *cruive* or *piggery*. A woodland pasture for pigs is a *droveden* or *denn*. Pigswill (or *mingle-mangle*) is *draff*, especially if it's from a brewery; it's eaten in a *stug*, or pig-trough. Nuts, especially acorns, used as food for pigs are called *mast*. When a pig has eaten a lot of *mast*, it's called *mastiff* or *masty* 'fat.'

A pig less than a year old is a *sheat*. A young weaned pig is a *shoat, speaning*, or *spaneling*. A young pig is also a *bonham*, a *boneen*, a *snork*, a *farrow*, a *gruntling*, a *grice*, or *griceling*. A young sow is a *gilt*. A boar less than two years old is a *sounder* or *hogget*. There are, not surprisingly, no terms for an old pig; pigs don't live to be old. They live to be bacon.

The smallest pig in the litter, the runt, is also called the *whinnock, tit-man, croot, reckling, wrig, rit, wreckling, wregling,* or *ritling.* A pig in heat is *brim,* and quite possibly *breme* 'fierce.'

A suckling pig baked whole in a pie is called *mermaid-pie.* If the pig is stuffed with forcemeat first, it's *enfarced.* If you're still hungry, *charlet* is a kind of custard of milk, eggs, and pork, and *smotheration* is a sailor's meal of beef and pork covered with potatoes. A dangerous-sounding pork dish is *Polony sausage,* which is served partially cooked. Small cakes of pork combined with lots of other ingredients (which remain unspecified) are called (or were called, the word is archaic) *raynolls.* Fat pork meat is called *speck,* especially in the United States and South Africa, and if pigs are

A pig in heat is *brim,* and quite possibly *breme* 'fierce.'

scarce the word can also be applied to the fat of a hippopotamus. But not, if you're kind, where the hippopotamus can overhear. Pork is also called *grunting-peck* or *grice,* and the lean part of the pig's loin is called *griskin.* A pig's hoof is a *cloot;* when it's cooked it's a *crubeen* or *pettitoes,* when pickled, *souse.* The ham or haunch of a pig, especially when eaten fresh, is called a *pestle.*

A common Scots proper name for a pig is *Grumphie* (used much the same way as *Spot* is for a dog). The *piggard* is set to watch Grumphie and the other pigs, and he rules in *pigdom,* the realm of pigs. If he does his job well, he's certain to end up a *piggicide.* If he's fat like a pig, he's a *porknell,* all the better to make him *long-pig:* human flesh from the cannibal's point of view.

peirastic an adjective meaning 'tentative, experimental.' From a Greek word meaning 'of the nature of trying.'

pelmatogram a high-flown word meaning 'footprint.' From a Greek word meaning 'sole of the foot.'

perissology an obsolete rhetorical term meaning 'redundancy of speech, pleonasm.' From a Greek word meaning 'speaking too much.'

phenology the study of the timing of recurring natural phenomena, such as volcanic explosion, rainfall and temperature variation, or the flowering times of plants. This word is an anglicization of a German word with the same meaning, taking the parts *pheno-* (as in *phenomenon*) and *-logical* (as in *meteorological*).

philostorgy natural affection, such as that between parents and children. From a Greek word meaning 'tenderly loving.'

photuria phosphorescence of the urine. From Greek roots meaning 'light' and 'urine,' but the real question is, how does this happen and how does one happen to find this out?

physitheism the deification of the weather. From Greek words meaning 'nature' and 'God.'

piacular a rare adjective meaning 'making or requiring atonement.' It comes from a Latin verb meaning 'to appease,' as does *expiate*, which means to atone or to make amends for one's wrongdoing.

pilgarlic a bald person, or a person who is held in humorous contempt or treated with mock pity. The word means 'peeled garlic.'

pilliver a pillowcase. From Old English words meaning 'pillow' and 'cover.' Another, more archaic synonym is *pillow-bere*.

pinguescence a rare word for the process of growing fat. It's also used loosely to mean obesity.

73

pinjrapol in India, a pen or enclosure where sick or old animals are kept.

piscation a rare word for fishing. A related term in English is *piscatorial,* meaning 'having to do with fishermen or fishing'; this is found mainly in formal writing, although it may also be used for humorous effect.

pishachi a female devil or ghost, especially one that dislikes travelers and pregnant women.

planeticose an adjective meaning 'liking to wander.' *Planet* comes from a Greek word meaning 'wanderer.'

plenisphere a perfect sphere. From a Latin word meaning 'full,' plus *sphere.*

plew a beaver skin. In former times, the skin of a beaver was used in Canada as a standard unit of value in the fur trade: the word comes from a Canadian French adjective meaning 'hairy.'

pluteus a shelf for books, small statues, etc. This comes from an identically spelled Latin word that originally meant 'a barrier or light wall between columns.'

pluviculture the science of making rain, or schemes for inducing rain. From a Latin word meaning 'rain,' on the model of *agriculture.*

poculiform an adjective meaning 'shaped like a cup.' The *-form* suffix, meaning 'having the shape of,' is remarkably productive, making it useful to people who can't bear to use a word like 'cup-shaped' when they could use a collateral adjective (one formed from a word collateral, or parallel, to the plain noun) instead. There's *drepaniform,* 'sickle-shaped,' *acetebuliform,* 'saucer-shaped,' *claviform,* 'club-shaped,' *hamiform,* 'hook-shaped,' *lacertiform,* 'lizard-shaped,' *moriform,* 'mulberry-shaped,' *patelliform,* 'kneecap-shaped,' *pugioniform,* 'dagger-shaped,' and *remiform,* 'oar-shaped.' Most of these words are used to describe the shapes of plant parts.

poffertje an Afrikaans word for a small doughnut dusted with sugar. The word ultimately comes from the French word *pouffer,* meaning 'to blow up.'

pogey an informal Canadian word meaning 'unemployment or welfare benefit,' as in "So you want me to end up on *pogey?*" It originally referred to a poorhouse or hostel for the needy or disabled: its current sense dates from the 1960s.

pok-ta-pok the Mayan name of a sacred ball game, also called *tlachtli* by the Aztecs. The object of the game was to put a rubber ball through a stone ring, using only hips, knees, and elbows.

pollinctor a person who prepares a dead body for cremation or embalming. A nice, important-sounding synonym for *Funeral Director.* This comes from a Latin word meaning 'to wash a corpse.'

polynya an area of open water in the middle of an expanse of ice, especially in the Arctic. This word comes from a Russian word for the same thing, which comes from a root meaning 'field.' The plural is *polynyi*, if you come across more than one.

polyonym the long-sought-after (almost-) synonym for *synonym*, it means 'each of a number of different words having the same meaning.' From a Greek word meaning 'having many names.'

pooking-fork a tool used in haymaking. It has a large prong and a cross handle, and it is used to push the hay into *pooks*, or stacks.

pooter a suction bottle for collecting insects and other small invertebrates. A *pooter* has one tube through which insects are drawn into the bottle and another, protected by muslin or gauze, which is sucked. It is apparently named after F. W. Poos (1891–1987), an American entomologist.

possident a rare term for a possessor, i.e., a person who owns something.

pregustator a person whose job it is to taste meats and drinks before serving them. From a Latin word meaning 'to taste before.'

pronk a weak or foolish person. This word is of uncertain origin, and it may come from a Dutch word meaning 'fop.' *Pronk* is also a verb used in South Africa of a springbok's leap in the air, especially as an alarm signal.

psilosopher a person with a petty or shallow philosophy. From the Greek root *psilo-*, meaning 'bare, mere.'

puku a colloquial New Zealand word meaning 'the stomach.' From a Maori word.

pulmentarious a rare word meaning 'made with gruel.'

pulsative an adjective applied to musical instruments, meaning 'played by percussion.' It can also be used to mean 'being able to throb or pulse,' as a heart.

pulsiloge an obsolete device, usually a pendulum, used to measure someone's pulse. It was formed by analogy with *horologe*, an older word for 'timepiece' or 'clock.'

pulveratricious an adjective meaning 'like birds that roll themselves in dust,' usually used as a fancy way of saying 'dust-colored.'

pyknic an adjective meaning 'stocky, with a rounded body and head, a thick trunk, and a tendency to fat.' It comes from a Greek word meaning 'thick,' and it was part of a system devised by Ernst Kretschmer (1888–1964) that correlated physical types with temperaments, criminal tendencies, and mental illness. The *pyknic* type was supposedly more prone to manic depression than the *leptosomic* (see **gammerstang**) type and tended towards crimes involving deception and fraud.

quaintrelle a well-dressed woman. A feminine form of a French word meaning 'beau, fop.'

qualtagh the first person you meet after leaving your house on some special occasion. Also, the first person entering a house on New Year's Day (often called a *first-foot*). The new year's *qualtagh*, for luck, is supposed to be a dark-haired man. A red-headed or female *qualtagh* is unlucky. Other things to bring luck to the house on New Year's Day include serving black-eyed peas, having the *qualtagh* bring shortbread and whiskey (sounds fine for any day of the year), and sweeping all the garbage in the house out through the front door before midnight on New Year's Eve (so that any of the misfortune of the past year is gone, not to return).

quangocrat a word found mostly in British English for a petty bureaucrat who works at a *Quasi-Autonomous Non-Governmental Organization* (or, acronymically, a *quango*).

quantophrenia an obsessive reliance on mathematical methods or results, especially in social science research where they may not be strictly applicable.

rassasy to satisfy a hungry person. This word is related to *satiate,* and they come from the same Latin root meaning 'enough.'

rastaquouère a social climber who tries too hard to be in fashion, especially one from a South American or Mediterranean country. Also, an exciting but untrustworthy stranger. From an American Spanish word meaning 'upstart.'

rawky a rare adjective which means 'foggy, damp, and cold,' as in *a rawky day* or *rawky weather.* It comes from *roke,* a dialect word for mist, fog, or drizzly rain.

retardataire an adjective meaning behind the times, or characteristic of an earlier period. Used mainly about artistic styles, it seems useful to describe people with fossilized hairdos: "She's so retardataire—when was the last time you saw a beehive like that?" The word comes from a French word meaning 'one who is late in arriving.'

retcon an often-condemned practice of writers for television and other serial stories, such as comic books, in which they mention previously unknown events in order to justify current plot points. The word is a blend of the words *retroactive* and *continuity.*

retrochoir not, as one might imagine, a group that only sings old church music, but instead the part of a cathedral or other large church that is behind the high altar.

retroition a rare word that means 'the action of returning; re-entrance.' Finally, a word for that embarrassing return to a party, after all good-byes have been said, to retrieve an essential item left behind (usually one's keys, making the retroition completely unavoidable).

rettery a place where flax is *retted*, or soaked and softened. Retting flax produces a very pungent, unpleasant odor, and *ret* and *rettery* are related to the word *rot*.

retund to blunt the sharp edge of a weapon, or to weaken something. A rare and obsolete word, it comes from a Latin word meaning 'to strike again.'

revolera a word for the fluttering of the cape above the matador's head. The more stereotypical bullfighting move of flapping the cape behind one's back is called *mariposa*, Spanish for 'butterfly.'

rhagades a plural noun meaning 'cracked or sore patches on the skin.' It comes from a Greek word meaning 'rent' (as in tear) or 'chink.'

rhathymia the state of being cheerful, merry, and optimistic. It comes from a Greek word meaning 'to take a vacation, be idle.'

rhedarious a rare adjective meaning 'used as a cart or chariot.' If you pile things on your wheeled office chair to move them down the hall, your chair is then *rhedarious*. It comes from a Latin word for a kind of four-wheeled carriage.

rhinarium the hairless and moist nose of some mammals.

savernapron a table-napkin. A corruption of an old French word meaning 'save-tablecloth.'

scamander to wander about. A rare word, it apparently comes from *Skamandros,* the name of a river in Homer's *Iliad.* Another, more familiar English word with the same meaning is *meander:* this is also based on the name of a river, a real one this time, the *Menderes,* known in ancient times as the *Maiandros.*

sciatherical an adjective meaning 'concerned with the recording of shadows, especially the shadow of the sun as a means for telling time.' From a Greek word for *sundial,* literally 'shadow-catcher.'

scibility an obsolete word meaning 'the power of knowing.' From a Latin word meaning 'able to know.'

scleragogy severe training or punishment of the body. From Greek roots meaning 'hard' and 'guiding.'

scofflaw someone who contemptuously breaks the law, especially a law that's difficult to enforce. This isn't a very rare word, but it has a marvelous origin. A Massachusetts man, Delcevare King of Quincy, held a contest in 1923 to find a word for the 'lawless drinker' of illegal alcohol, and he offered $200 as a prize. He received 25,000 entries, coming from all over the United States and from several foreign countries. Two entrants, Mr. Henry Irving Dale and Miss Kate L. Butler, independently came up with *scofflaw,* and they split the prize on January 15, 1924.

scrimshandrix a rare word meaning a woman who makes scrimshaw (carvings on ivory or bone, often done by sailors). The masculine term is *scrimshander;* another term in use (or as much use as it can hope to get) is *scrimshoner,* and the process of making scrimshaw can be called *scrimshonting.* The origin of the word isn't known, but it may have come from the name *Scrimshaw.*

scripophily the collecting of stock and bond certificates, not as investments, but as works of art or because of the issuing company's historical or economic significance. The word comes from *scrip,* a word for a stock certificate, and *-phily.*

scrippage one's baggage and personal belongings. William Shakespeare invented the word, using it in the phrase 'scrip and scrippage,' on the pattern of 'bag and baggage'; a *scrip* was a small bag or pouch carried by a pilgrim, shepherd, or beggar.

selcouth an adjective meaning 'unfamiliar, rare, strange, marvelous, wonderful.' It comes from Old English words meaning 'seldom known.' *Uncouth* and *selcouth* used to be synonyms, but *uncouth* now means 'unpleasant, rude.' Another rare, etymologically overdetermined word meaning 'rare' is *rarachose,* which comes from French *rare chose,* 'rare thing.'

semiopathy the tendency to read humorously inappropriate meanings into signs. One anecdote is about the literary critic Terry Eagleton (1943–). He saw a sign next to an escalator reading "Dogs Must Be Carried." Since he wanted to go upstairs, he went off to find a dog. Other fine examples are "Slow Children Crossing" and "The Door Is Alarmed." The word seems to have been coined by the editors of the "Feedback" section of *New Scientist* magazine.

seplasiary a perfumer. This word comes from the name of a street in Capua in Southern Italy where perfume was sold.

sericipiary an adjective meaning 'producing silk,' from Latin roots meaning 'silk' and 'birth.'

sericon a substance supposed to be involved in the process of changing base metals into gold. Obviously, there is no basis for connecting this substance with zinc, which was done by some writers of the eighteenth century.

sermocination an extremely irritating rhetorical device in which the speaker, having asked a question, immediately answers it. The words *sermocinator* and *sermocinatrix* mean 'speaker' and 'female speaker,' respectively.

shamal a hot, dry, north-westerly wind blowing across the Persian Gulf in summer and typically causing sandstorms. The term comes from the Arabic word for 'north.' The *simoom* is another hot, dry wind that blows in this part of the world: it takes its name from an Arabic word meaning 'to poison.'

siagonology the study of jawbones, especially in order to deduce personality traits or racial characteristics. From a Greek root meaning 'jaw.'

sindonology the study of the Shroud of Turin.

sitooterie a summerhouse or gazebo; also an out-of-the-way corner to sit with your partner during a dance. The word means 'a place to sit out' and comes from *sit* plus *oot* (Scots pronunciation of 'out') and the noun ending *-erie*.

sleck soft mud, ooze. *Sleck* is supposedly finer and smoother than sludge to the discerning mind (or foot).

snollygoster a dishonest politician, especially a shrewd or calculating one. A connection has been proposed between this word and *snallygaster*, a mythical monster of Maryland, invented to frighten freed slaves. However, the first evidence for *snallygaster* follows *snollygoster* by about a hundred years, making a connection (in this direction, at least) unlikely.

solander a protective box, made in the form of a book, for holding items such as botanical specimens, maps, and color plates. The word comes from the name of Daniel C. Solander, an eighteenth-century Swedish botanist.

solein an adjective meaning 'done alone, in privacy or solitude.' A lonesome-sounding word, it comes from the same root as *sole,* and the word *sullen* is descended from it. It seems that if you do too much alone, you become sullen.

spumescence foaminess, frothiness.

SQUINTIFEGO

squassation a severe shaking. From an Italian word with the same meaning.

squintifego a person who squints very much.

squirk a half-suppressed laugh. Of imitative origin.

starchitect a star architect. Usually used derisively, as in "The defining characteristic of the *starchitects* is their utter disregard for the laws of physics and the people who will actually use the building."

steganography the art of secret writing; cryptography. This word is now usually used to mean the practice of hiding secret data by encoding it electronically in another, innocuous file. Sometimes it's abbreviated as *stego*. How is it related to the other *stego*, the *stegosaurus*? They both come from a Greek word meaning 'covered.' In *steganography*, the writing is covered up; the *stegosaurus* is covered in bony plates.

stelk a dish made of onions and mashed potatoes, with a large lump (often an entire pound) of butter or lard in the middle of it. It's an Irish dish and is also called *champ*.

stellionate a legal term for fraud committed in making contracts, especially that which involves selling the same thing (or rights to the same thing) to different persons, often a thing that is not the fraudster's possession to begin with. So, not just selling the Brooklyn Bridge, but selling it twice. This comes from a Latin word meaning 'a fraudulent person' and may be derived from a word for a kind of lizard.

steracle an obsolete word meaning 'a spectacle or show.' This word may come from the word *stare*, modeled on *spectacle*.

STOOP-GALLANT

sternutation the act of sneezing or a sneeze. From a Latin word with the same meaning, this word is used mostly in medical contexts, or by people trying to be funny. Something that causes sneezing is *sternutatory;* a medicine that causes sneezing is *errhine.*

stoop-gallant a disease or illness. A historical term, it originally referred specifically to the sweating sicknesses prevalent in England in the fifteenth and sixteenth centuries and is presumably meant to suggest that such illnesses would bring 'gallants,' i.e., fine gentlemen, to their knees with weakness and exhaustion.

stylite a Christian ascetic who lived standing on top of a pillar in ancient times, permanently exposed to the elements, and dependent on others for food and drink brought up by ladder. The word comes from *stulos,* the Greek for *pillar,* and the first and best-known *stylite,* or *pillar saint,* was St. Simeon Stylites, who spent thirty years living in this way.

superbious a very rare adjective meaning 'proud and overbearing.' It comes from a Latin word meaning 'proud or magnificent,' as does the familiar English adjective *superb.*

supputation the act of computing or calculating. From a Latin word meaning 'count up.'

sychnocarpous an adjective meaning 'bearing fruit many times.'

sycomancy divination by means of figs or fig-leaves.

taniwha a mythical monster that, according to Maori legend, lives in very deep water.

tappen the plug by which the rectum of a bear is closed during hibernation: according to J. G. Wood in an 1865 volume of *Illustrated Natural History,* 'the tappen is almost entirely composed of pine-leaves, and the various substances which the Bear scratches out of the ants's nests.' There is no contemporary evidence of the word's use and no further information to be found regarding the composition of the plug!

tegestology the collecting of beer mats. Irregularly formed from a Latin word meaning 'covering, mat.'

telautograph a forgotten offshoot of the telegraph in which writing done with a pen or pencil at the transmitter is reproduced at the receiving end by communicating movements to the receiving pen. There are no citations in the *OED* after 1905. From a Greek root meaning 'distance' and *autograph.*

tellurian an adjective meaning 'of or inhabiting the earth.' The word is also used as a noun to mean 'an inhabitant of the earth,' especially in science fiction: it comes from a Latin word meaning 'the earth.'

telmatology the study of peat-bogs. The adjective for *peat-boggian,* if needed, is *turbarian,* and the Scottish dialect word for *peat-bog* is *yarpha.*

TEMULENT

... so I sez to him, I sez, you think you're so great because you got the big ossif, and I got the little ossif? Well, you know what? Everybody hates your guffs, thass what...

telpherage a system where minerals or other goods are transported in buckets suspended from a cable and moved by an electric motor supplied with current from an adjacent conductor. From Greek roots meaning 'distance' and 'bearing.'

temulent an adjective meaning 'drunken' or 'intoxicating,' from Latin roots meaning 'intoxicating drink' and 'wine.'

tendsome a possibly imaginary word, supposedly meaning 'requiring much attendance.' This is a word that is only known through dictionary entries; two from Webster (in 1847 and 1864) and one from the *Century Dictionary* (1891). Not that lexicographers ever put in words maliciously, but occasionally a word that looks all right will slip through, like an uninvited guest. And, with words as with people, once they're seen in the right crowd, other parties (and other dictionaries) become open to them.

thalassic an adjective meaning 'relating to the sea,' from the Greek for sea, *thalassa.* Many of today's health and beauty centers offer *thalassotherapy,* which is the use of seawater for various therapeutic and cosmetic purposes.

thelytokous an adjective meaning 'producing only female offspring.' It is usually used to refer to the offspring of parthenogenesis, but there's no reason why its meaning can't be extended to the offspring of more conventional conception. From Greek roots meaning 'bearing' and 'female.' The word for having only male offspring is *arrenotokous.*

theopneust an adjective meaning 'divinely inspired.' From Greek roots meaning 'God' and 'breathe.'

therblig in time and motion study, any task that can be analyzed. This is an anagram of the name *Gilbreth*, from F. B. Gilbreth, an American engineer who was very influential in the field of motion study. (His children wrote two books about growing up in the home of a motion-study expert: *Cheaper by the Dozen* and *Belles on Their Toes*.)

thixotropy the property of certain gels of becoming liquid when agitated and turning into a gel again when allowed to stand. From a German word with the same meaning, from Greek roots meaning 'touching' and 'turning.'

thwarterous an adjective meaning 'twisted, gnarled.' A nonce-word irregularly formed from *thwart* on the model of *boisterous*.

tigon the hybrid offspring of a male tiger and a lion. A *liger* is the offspring produced by a male lion and a tigress.

titivil a name for a devil said to collect words mumbled, dropped, or omitted in the recitation of divine service, and to carry them to hell where they would be held against the offender. By extension, a *tattletale*.

tmesis the separation of the parts of a compound word by the interposition of another word or words. From a Greek root meaning 'cutting.' The *OED* gives the example, 'How bright the chit and chat!'

tokoloshe in African folklore, a mischievous and lascivious hairy water sprite. The word comes from the Sesotho, Xhosa, and Zulu languages, and it's pronounced "TOKolosh."

Torschlusspanik a German word (one of those concepts, like *Schadenfreude* or *Sprachgefühl* that English, too lazy to come up with an Anglo-Saxon word, appropriates the German for) meaning 'a sense of panic in middle age brought on by the feeling that life is passing you by.' It literally means 'shut door panic.'

tracasserie a state of annoyance or a petty quarrel. This comes from a French word meaning 'to worry oneself.' A citation in the *OED* from 1879 reads "Life seems to me empty of all but *tracasseries*."

tractatrix a female shampooer. It is not recommended that you ask for the services of such a person by this term at your beauty parlor, salon, or barbershop, to avoid embarrassing misunderstandings.

tragelaph a fictional beast that was part goat and part stag. From Greek roots meaning 'he-goat' and 'stag.'

tragematopolist a deservedly rare word meaning 'a seller of candy.' From a Greek word meaning 'dried fruit or candy.'

tralatitious an adjective meaning 'traditional, handed down from generation to generation.' From a Latin word meaning 'usual.'

trental thirty requiem masses (said on the same day or on different days) or the payment for saying them. Also, any set of thirty things, or a service said on the thirtieth day after burial. From a Latin root meaning 'thirty.'

trillibub the entrails of an animal, especially in the phrase *tripes and trillibubs* or *tricks and trillibubs*. The etymology of this word is obscure (as are the entrails themselves).

trilling one of a set of three, especially one of a set of triplets; a triplet.

tripotage pawing, handling, or fingering, especially of people.

tripudiant dancing; used figuratively to mean 'triumphant, exultant.' The *tripudium* was a ritual dance of ancient Rome, done by armed priests. The dance involved three steps (*tripudium* means 'three feet') and included banging on shields with rods or spears.

tristichous arranged in three rows or ranks. A *tristich* is a group of three lines of poetry or a stanza of three lines; a *distich* is a couplet. They all come from a Greek word meaning 'row.'

troke an obsolete word meaning 'to fail, to be unable to do something' or 'to deceive.' This word comes from an Old English word whose derivation is not known.

tropology the use of metaphors in writing or speaking. To *tropologize* something is to use it as a metaphor, for instance "He was the John Wayne of the grease pit."

truchmanry the office of an interpreter. The word *dragoman*, meaning 'interpreter,' is related etymologically—they both come from an Arabic word meaning 'interpreter.'

trypall a tall, lanky, slovenly person. See **gammerstang**.

tsantsa a human head shrunk as a war trophy by the Jivaros of Ecuador in South America. The word comes from the language of this people and is pronounced as it is spelled.

turngiddy an adjective meaning 'dizzy from spinning around.' If you spend too long *turngiddy*, you might get *turn-sick*, another word for 'dizzy.'

tuyere the nozzle through which a blast of air is forced into a forge or furnace. It has also been called a *tew-iron* or a *twire-pipe*.

twitter-light an obsolete word meaning 'twilight.' It has what to modern ears is an uglier cousin, *twatter-light*.

tykhana in India, an underground place to rest in during the hottest part of the day. It comes from an Urdu word meaning 'nether house.'

typhlology the scientific knowledge relating to blindness, from Greek *typhlo-*, meaning 'blind,' and *-logy*, meaning 'science of.'

typocrat one who rules by controlling the press. This word was made from *typo-*, meaning 'type,' and the suffix *-crat* on the model of words like *democrat*. A related *typo-* word is *typomania*, the overwhelming desire to see one's name in print.

ubiation the act of occupying a new place. From a Latin word meaning 'where.' *Ubication* is the condition of being in a certain place, and *ubity* is a rare word meaning 'place.'

ugsomeness a word meaning 'loathing,' which at one time also meant ugliness or 'the quality of being *ugsome*' or horrible. *Uglyography* is an invented word meaning 'bad handwriting or uncouth spelling.'

ultra-crepidarian an adjective related to the (widespread) practice of giving opinions on topics beyond one's knowledge. The word comes from Latin words meaning 'beyond the sole (of the shoe),' an allusion to the story of Apelles and the cobbler, Apelles being the favorite painter of Alexander the Great. His shoemaker told him of a mistake Apelles had made in depicting a shoe, and Apelles corrected it. The shoemaker then presumed to criticize the painting of the leg as well, and Apelles said: "Don't criticize above the sole!"

ultrafidian an adjective meaning 'blindly credulous.' It comes from the Latin phrase *ultra fidem* 'beyond faith.'

undaftiness untidiness. The word associated with the 'tidy' part is not *daft* 'silly,' but the dialect word *deft,* meaning 'tidy, pretty.'

UTRICIDE

undern an early meaning was 'the third hour of the day' (meant to be about nine o'clock). Later, confusingly, the sixth hour of the day, or midday, and the afternoon or evening. A wonderful word to use when you know you will be late but don't want to admit it: "See you about *undern!*" It can also mean a meal eaten at midday or in the afternoon.

upaithric an adjective meaning 'having no roof' (usually intentionally, so as to see the stars). A synonym is *hypaethral,* and both words come from a Greek word meaning 'under the sky.'

upbrixle upbraid, scold. An obsolete word related to *upbraid.*

usucaption in law, the acquisition of ownership of a place from having continuous undisturbed or uninterrupted possession. From a Latin law term of the same meaning.

utraquism a rare word meaning 'the use of two languages on an equal basis.' From a Latin phrase meaning 'under each kind.'

utricide a person who stabs an inflated vessel of skin. The citations in the *OED* give no clue as to why someone would want to do this (other than to hear the pleasing "pop!"). It comes from a Latin word that means 'a leather bottle.'

uxorilocal an adjective meaning 'living in or near the wife's home or community after marriage.' Living near the husband's home is *virilocal.* Another related word is *matrilocal.* It's a synonym for *uxorilocal,* not a word for that butt of frequent jokes, a person living at home with his or her mother.

105

vagarious a rare word meaning 'erratic and unpredictable in behavior or direction.' Its ultimate origin is a Latin verb meaning 'to wander,' and this also gave rise to the English word *vagary*, an unexpected and inexplicable change in a situation or in someone's behavior.

vappa a rare word meaning 'flat or sour wine.' This word has also been used to mean 'a state of the blood when it is in a low, dispirited condition.'

vapulatory an adjective meaning 'relating to flogging.' Unsurprisingly, it comes from a Latin word meaning 'to be beaten.'

varve a pair of thin layers of clay and silt of contrasting color and texture that represent the deposit of a single year (summer and winter) in a lake at some time in the past, usually in a lake formed by a retreating ice sheet. The word comes from a Swedish word meaning 'layer.'

vaticinate to predict events; to speak as a prophet. A rarer adjective from the same Latin root is *vaticinant*, meaning 'prophesying.'

vease a run before a leap. The word is often (well, as often as such a word as this can expect) spelled *feeze* or *pheese*, especially in the United States. A quotation in the *OED* from 1675 reads "If a man do but goe back a little to take his *feeze*, he may easily jump over it."

veilleuse a small and highly decorated nightlight. Also, for those fond of midnight snacks, a bedside food-warmer.

verecund an adjective meaning 'shy, coy, bashful.' Other words that end in -*cund* are the familiar *fecund*, 'fruitful,' *irecund*, 'passionate, angry,' and *namecund*, 'famous.' However, these words are not closely related etymologically. A word that is related to *verecund* etymologically is *vergoynous*, 'ashamed.'

vermian a rare adjective meaning 'worm-like,' based on the Latin word for *worm*. Related words in English include *vermicide*, a substance that is poisonous to worms, and *vermivorous*, feeding on worms.

viduous a rare adjective meaning 'empty.' William Makepeace Thackeray (1811–1863) uses this word to describe a heart as a 'viduous mansion' for rent after the loved one is gone, going on to say that the new tenant finds a miniature, or portrait, of the first love hidden away somewhere within it.

vigenary an adjective meaning 'of or relating to the number twenty.' From the Latin word for 'twenty.' A *vicenary* was a person who commanded twenty other people.

vigoro an Australian team game for women, with elements of baseball and cricket, played with a soft rubber ball.

viliority a rare word meaning 'the fact of being cheaper or of less value.' From a Latin root meaning 'to make viler.'

vimineous a rare adjective meaning 'made of wicker.' From a Latin word meaning 'willow.'

vindemy the taking of honey from beehives. From a Latin word meaning 'fruit-gathering.'

voisinage an obsolete word meaning 'neighborhood,' related to *vicinity*. It can also mean 'the fact of being near,' usually applied only to places, but ready for an extended figurative meaning such as "He was overcome by the *voisinage* of his beloved."

voulu an adjective meaning 'contrived, affected, deliberate.' The word comes from a French word meaning 'to wish, to want,' and it seems to have had a vogue in the early part of the twentieth century, used by such writers as Elizabeth Bowen (1899–1973) and Lawrence Durrell (1912–1990).

wabbit a Scottish word meaning 'exhausted or slightly unwell,' as in "I'm feeling a bit *wabbit*." Its origin is uncertain.

waff a Scottish word meaning 'a slight blow, as in passing' or 'a slight touch of illness.' A very useful word, it can also mean 'a glimpse,' 'a wraith,' 'a whiff of perfume,' and 'a waving movement of the hand or something held in the hand.'

weddinger a wedding guest; also, the entire wedding party, including the bride and groom.

weesle a very rare, undeservedly obsolete word meaning 'to ooze.'

widdendream an obsolete Scottish word meaning 'in a state of confusion or mental disturbance,' often in the phrase *in a widdendream*. From an Old English phrase meaning 'in mad joy.'

winebibber a person who habitually drinks a lot of alcohol. The word was coined by Miles Coverdale (1488–1568) in his translation of the first complete printed English Bible: "Kepe no company with *wyne bebbers* and ryotous eaters of flesh" (Proverbs 23:20). It is rarely used today except for humorous effect.

woofits an unwell feeling, especially a headache; a moody depression; a hangover. In one citation this is called "that dread disease that comes from overeating and underdrinking" and "the ailment that comes with 'the morning after the night before.'"

wootz a kind of very tough and sharp steel made in southern India by fusing magnetic iron ore with material containing carbon. Apparently this is a misprint for *wook*.

worble an obsolete Scottish word meaning 'to wriggle or wallow.' Its origin is obscure but it may be related to the word *wrabble*, which also means 'to wriggle.'

XESTURGY

xenization a rare word meaning 'the fact of traveling as a stranger.' It comes from a Greek word meaning 'to entertain strangers' or 'to be a stranger.'

xenology the scientific study of extraterrestrial phenomena. Mainly used in science fiction, the term comes from a Greek word meaning 'strange': other English words that are based on this root include *xenophobia,* the intense or irrational dislike or fear of people from other countries, and *xenotransplantation,* the grafting or transplanting of organs or tissues between members of different species.

xesturgy an obsolete and rare word meaning 'the process of polishing.' From a Greek word meaning 'to polish.'

xu a monetary unit of Vietnam, formally abandoned in 1986, equaling one hundredth of a dong. The word comes from the French *sou.*

xylophory a rare word meaning 'wood-carrying,' from a Greek word with the same meaning. The Feast of Tabernacles is a Jewish holiday that was once called the *festival of xylophory* (now called *Sukkot*), which is celebrated by building a sukkah (a ceremonial temporary shelter) in which all meals are eaten for the seven days of the festival. The roof of the sukkah is supposed to be made of something that grew from the ground and was cut off, usually branches (or any wood), corn, or bamboo.

EXCEPTIONAL AND EXTRAORDINARY X-ES

X the unknown, *X* the mysterious,

X the secret factor, *X* marks the spot . . . there's something about a word that starts with *X* that demands a second glance. And maybe a third, with some surreptitious scribbling to make sure you've got the spelling right.

Because *X* is rarer than we'd like, quite a few of the snazziest *X*-words revolve around just a few roots. *Xantho-*, from a Greek word meaning 'yellow,' is one of them. There are the *Xanthochroi,* one of Thomas Henry Huxley's (1825–1895) varieties of humanity, with their smooth yellow hair and pale complexions—also called *xanthous.*

Xeno/a- is another one of these roots, from a Greek word meaning 'foreigner,' 'stranger,' or 'guest.' There's *xenagogue,* a fancy word for 'tour guide,' and *xenagogy,* a fancy word for 'guide book.' A *xenodochium* is a hostel, especially one in a monastery, and *xenodochy* 'hospitality' is what you would expect to find there. *Xenization* is the act of traveling as a stranger. Something that is *xenogeneic* is descended from an individual of a different species—pretty handy for those long discussions of the consequences of alien abductions.

A scientific root meaning 'dry,' *xero-*, is also Greek, and shows up in several *X*-words, including *xerophagy,* 'the eating of dry food, especially as a form of fasting,' and *xerotine siccative* 'a substance used to dry ships'

bottoms' (presumably from the inside). Those dry bottoms were probably made of wood, and wood also has an *x*-root, *xylo-*. *Xylography* is wood-engraving, especially of the cruder sort, or printing from wood blocks. Something that is *xylophagous* eats wood, like some insect larvae, or destroys wood, as some mollusks do. A *xoanon* is a crudely shaped image

or statue of a deity, often made of wood, but it is related to the Greek root for 'scrape, carve,' like *xyster*, an instrument for scraping bones (used in a surgical, not a culinary, way). Once the bones are scraped, you could subject them to *xesturgy*, the process of polishing. You could then wrap the whole thing up in *xilinous* bandages—ones made of cotton.

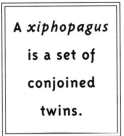

A *xiphopagus* is a set of conjoined twins.

A *xiphopagus* is a set of conjoined twins linked by a band of tissue extending from the *xiphoid* cartilage. Both of these words come from a Greek word meaning 'sword.'

X can also stand for any number of things, such as the well-known Roman numeral, the *XXX* movie, and the algebraic unknown, but also as *xr*, 'December,' *x* 'ten-dollar bill' and *XX* 'twenty-dollar bill.'

One last note about the letter we call "ex"—the Romans called it "ix" instead. Either way, it's excellent.

yaffle an English dialect name for the green woodpecker. It originated in the late eighteenth century, apparently in imitation of the bird's characteristic laughing call; in some parts of Britain it's also known as a *yaffingale*.

zedonk the offspring of a male zebra and a female donkey, if such a pair is allowed to express their forbidden love. It is also known as a *zonkey* or *zeedonk,* and citations suggest one was born in the (obviously open-minded) Prospect Park Zoo in Brooklyn, New York, in 1973.

zetetic a rare word meaning 'proceeding by inquiry or investigation.' It comes from a Greek verb meaning 'to seek.'

ziraleet an expression of joy by a group of women in Aleppo, consisting of the words "Lillé, Lillé, Lillé" repeated as often as possible in one breath. Also used figuratively for any expression of joy.

zopissa a medicinal preparation made from wax and pitch scraped from the sides of ships: fortunately the substance is no longer in use, so the word is obsolete. It came from a Greek word for pitch, a sticky resinous substance obtained from tar or turpentine.

Zyrian a former term for Komi, a language spoken by a people living in an area of northern Russia west of the Urals. This is currently the last entry in the *OED.*

HOW TO CREATE YOUR OWN WEIRD AND WONDERFUL WORDS

Every word in English had to start with a person trying to express a thought. As far as we know, none of the words in the English language were brought to the planet by aliens, borrowed from dolphins or whales, or dug up on ancient tablets of unknown provenance. Each and every word was first spoken or written by a person who had to create the word from their own store of sounds and roots.

In almost every case, that inventive person is anonymous. Most words were probably independently created by many different people over a wide area, and can't be traced to a particular writer or speaker. There are some exceptions: Gelett Burgess is said to have coined the word *blurb* 'a short description of a book or other product used for promotional purposes.' *Hotsy-totsy* 'just right' was coined in 1926 by Billie De Beck, an American cartoonist. *Nylon* was coined by DuPont chemists. And *yester-year*, which sounds ancient, was actually coined in 1870 by Dante Gabriel Rosetti, who needed it to aptly translate a French word.

The great majority of coined words, however, are for scientific and technical things. If you have created, discovered, researched, found, developed, or simply predicted the existence of a thing or idea, naturally you'd like to name it. Thus we have the chemical elements *neptunium* (from the planet Neptune: neptunium is just after uranium in the periodic table and Neptune is just after Uranus) and *rubidium* (from a Latin word meaning 'red' because is has red lines in its spectrum). We have tiny organisms, such as *Salmonella* and *rickettsia* (both named after people—Ricketts died because of his work with these parasites) and bigger organisms, like the *allosaurus* (whose name means 'other lizard') and the *Cnidaria* (whose name comes from a Greek word meaning 'nettle,' and oddly enough, they sting!). There are specialized terms in the social sciences, like *etic* (coined by the phoneticist Kenneth Pike, to describe a generalized approach to the structure of language) and *intertextual* (coined by Julia Kristeva: 'denoting literary criticism that considers a text in the light of its relation to other texts'), *subliminal* (coined in the early 1800s, 'below the threshold of sensation or consciousness') and *amusia* (which sounds funnier than it actually is: 'condition in which there is the loss of a musical ability'). *Ornithopter, oogonium,* and *drogulus* are other examples of weird and wonderful coined words. (Determining their meanings is left as an exercise in dictionary use for the reader.)

By this time, you're probably itching to jump in and do a little coining yourself. Although English has no Committee or Academy or Board that reviews new words for suitability and usefulness, there are a few loose rules that tend to work on their own either for or against the widespread adoption of a new word.

The first of these loose rules is unwritten, but not unspoken. It's the rule of pronounceability. Sure, *xzyqt* looks grand, but how do you say it? Be sure to include plenty of vowels in your coinages. Also, it's a good idea to make sure that contiguous consonant sounds are easy to say together. *Adtim* is certain to be pronounced "adim" or "atim," because it's very difficult to correctly enunciate a *d* followed by a *t* and keep them both separate. A handy chart of the sounds of English and the various ways they can be spelled appears on the opposite page.

Sound	Possible Spellings	Sound	Possible Spellings
æ	hat, plaid, calf, laugh, Cheyenne	n	nod, banner, knot, gnat, pneumatic
ā	page, maid, day, freight, skein, hey, steak, valet, straight, gauge, café, soiree	NG	strong, pink, meringue, handkerchief
ä	father, heart, ah, balm, guard, yacht, baa, encore, reservoir, lot	ō	only, goal, grow, soul, doe, brooch, dough, folk, chateau, oh, chauffeur, owe, sew, Seoul, depot, apropos
b	bed, babble		
CH	church, suture, patch, digestion, righteous, cello, Czech, catsup	ô	fall, audio, law, fought, talk, caught, cough, awe, Utah, broad
d	dad, milled, odd		
e	mend, dread, many, said, friend, jeopardy, says, heifer, bury	oi	oil, toy, buoy, lawyer
		ŏŏ	pull, wood, amour, wolf, could, Rwanda
ē	equal, funny, eagle, tree, ski, believe, either, key, algae, Phoenix, people, buoy, debris	ōō	mood, mule, prove, pooh, group, sue, pew, suit, canoe, maneuver, through, adieu, buoy, debut, coup
er	care, pair, aerial, there, prayer, their, bear, heirloom		
ə	occur, about, April, mother, cautious, circus, oxygen, bargain, dungeon, tortoise, pageant, aurora	ow	pout, fowl, bough, hour, Saudi, Mao
		p	pan, happen
f	fan, giraffe, graph, tough	r	rat, marry, wrath, rhyme
g	get, giggle, rogue, guess, ghoul, exist	s	sat, cement, dense, trance, kiss, scene, listen, psycho, blitz, sword
h	her, whole, Gila monster, jicama, Oaxaca	SH	short, station, social, fission, tension, machine, tissue, ocean, schwa, sure
i	fin, elastic, gym, manage, ear, guild, sieve, busy, women, marriage, been, weird	t	tent, matter, stopped, debt, two, thyme, pterodactyl, pizza
ī	ice, fly, pie, high, rye, sign, eye, island, height, either, bayou, kaiser, aisle, aye, guy, Cheyenne, coyote, annihilate, guide	TH	thin
		T̲H̲	there, breathe
		v	vest, pave, of
j	jar, gent, charge, fudge, legion, gradual, badge, soldier, exaggerate	w	win, wheat, quit, choir, croissant, Nahuatl
		y	yet, onion, accuse, hallelujah, azalea
k	kin, cup, tack, chemist, ache, account, excite, quick, opaque, liquor, lacquer, Sikh, saccharin	z	zip, musician, fuzz, scissors, ruse, xylophone, clothes, raspberry, asthma, czar
l	let, bell, tale, pedal, tunnel, lentil		
m	men, summon, palm, limb, damn, paradigm	ZH	vision, treasure, massage, azure, regime, equation, nausea

Choose your sounds wisely, then choose the spelling of them. Avoid spellings that have too many possible sounds. Consider *mallough:* is it "maloo" or "maluff"?

You may also want to consider using a simple spelling as opposed to a more complicated or fancy one. No one likes a silent letter, even when deployed for humorous or allusive reasons. (Old joke: Q: how do you pronounce Hen3ry? A: "Hen-ree."—The "3" is silent.) If your word is too difficult to spell, people will avoid it out of fear or irritation. Tied in with spelling is the ease of writing the word conventionally. If your word has internal punctuation (such as *ca!met* or *we?zem*) you can pretty much forget about seeing it used widely. (These characters also present a pronunciation problem.) This also applies to inventing your own alphabetic characters. Very few people will want to add a new character to their font sets just to be able to use your new word.

One way to get around spelling and pronunciation problems is to co-opt an existing word and give it a new meaning, rather than attempting to achieve a novel arrangement of letters and sounds. This is how much slang is made. *Lettuce, dough, bread*—all can mean 'money,' now. Inventing slang is a little beyond the scope of this essay. However, if you're determined to create an entirely new word and have thought about the pronunciation and spelling pitfalls, here are a few easy steps.

1. Decide whether you care if your word is *macaronic* or not. A macaronic word takes parts from two or more different languages: a Latin root and a Greek suffix, perhaps. In the word-coining world, a little more credibility is given to words that take all their parts from just one language. They're seen as more sincere.

However, this isn't a hard-and-fast distinction, and it is one that you can safely ignore if you're not inclined to be a purist.

2. Either choose your meaning and look for parts, or choose your parts and look for meaning. Either way, there's a handy list of roots, suffixes, and prefixes here for you to use. If you're dying to have a new word that means "overly eager to speak" you might look for roots *acer* 'fierce, eager' and *dicto* 'to speak', and then add a suffix that makes adjectives, like *-ous,* to get *acerdictous.* (Take care that your suffixes correspond to the part of speech you want. *Acerdictous* doesn't sound like a noun, so it would be odd in: "He's so *acerdictous* that he took over the whole meeting.") If you are fond of the parts *bathy-* 'relating to depth' and *-ster* 'a person engaged in or associated with a particular activity or thing' you might be tempted to fiddle around until you got *bathyster* 'a particularly deep person.' If you don't find parts for the meaning you want, find a dictionary with good etymologies and look up words that have meanings close to the meaning you want. Avoid ordinary words. For instance, if you're looking for a part that means 'angry,' don't look up *angry.* Look up *irate.* That gets you the Latin root *ira* 'anger.' Can't think of a fancier word for what you want? Use a thesaurus.

3. Don't feel as if you have to use Latin and Greek roots. You may have just as much success merging "ordinary" words. *Humongous* (probably from *huge* and *monstrous)* and *ginormous* (*gigantic + enormous*) are two similar and fairly recent words

that are rearrangements of other more ordinary words, instead of meldings of Latin and Greek roots or blendings of roots plus ordinary words.

4. Be practical. It's easier for a new word to gain acceptance if it denotes something for which we don't already have a handy word. Trying to convince people to use your word *kwillum* 'wall' when we already have the word *wall* is a lost cause. If *kwillum* means 'wall being fought over by neighbors' you have a better chance.

5. Once you have a word, try it out on a few people. (I suggest trying it out with your family and friends before unleashing it on your boss or teachers.) Practice saying it several times by yourself. If the pronunciation doesn't come trippingly off your tongue, add sounds where necessary. English is pretty forgiving of the 'uh' sound (often called schwa, represented by ə) and can insert it almost anywhere. Can't say *dreklistic* easily? Try *drekilistic*. Use your new word in informal letters and e-mail and particularly in appropriate postings to Internet forums. If by chance you have the opportunity to be published in traditional media, weigh it carefully as a means of word dissemination. Make sure that the published piece is the right setting for your new word, in both tone and subject matter. You wouldn't introduce a new scientific term in a humorous essay, and a humorous new word might be somewhat out of place in a report on a new scientific discovery.

6.   Be patient. It can take years or decades for a new word to be accepted by a majority of speakers. You may not ever see your creation in a dictionary, especially if it was a word created just for a single use or publication (these are called *nonce-words,* and they don't make it into most dictionaries). The joy of having created a word, a word of your very own, should be enough. Do not send your new word to dictionary editors, unless it has been used in major print sources (not just on the Internet or in local or specialist publications) more than a dozen times, by people other than yourself. Anything less than that isn't worth your time or the dictionary editor's.

One last note before you begin: once you have your new word, you might want to look it up in the largest dictionary you can find (I suggest, of course, the *OED)* and online with one or two search engines. You may find that your shiny new word is in fact sporting a fine patina, having been coined already centuries back, or even last week. Something that can be thought probably has been thought, and quite likely already subjected to logopoeia or verbifaction. Good luck!

How to Create Your Own

acer- fierce, eager

agro-, agri- of or involving agriculture

ana-, an- up; back; again

-androus having male parts

ante- before; in front

apo- away from; separate

arch- chief; principal

astro- of stars or space

auto-, aut- self; spontaneous

bathy-, batho- of or relating to depth

brachy-, -brach short

cata-, cat-, kata- down(ward); wrongly or badly; completely; against

cephalo- -headed

chiro-, cheiro- of the hand or hands

chrys-, chryso- of or relating to gold

circum- around; about

clado-, clad- of or relating to a branch or branching

copro- of or relating to dung or feces

-crat denoting a member or supporter of a form of government or rule

cyno- of or relating to dogs

dicto- speak

-drome denoting a place for running or racing

dys- bad; difficult

ecto- outer; external

eu- good; well; easily

-facient producing a specified action or state

-gony denoting a kind of origin or reproduction

-gram denoting something written or recorded

gymno-, gymn- naked

gyneco- of or relating to women

hiero-, hier- sacred; holy

ideo- of or relating to an idea or form

idio- distinct; private; personal

infra- below or under

lepto-, lept- small; narrow

logo- of or relating to words

mal- unpleasantly; badly; improperly; not -

mero- partly; partial

-monger dealer or trader; promoter of some activity or feeling

-morph, -morphic having, denoting, or relating

-nomy an area of knowledge or the laws governing it

oligo-, olig- having or involving few

para-, par- beside or adjacent to; analogous to

peri- round or about; nearest

philo-, phil-, -phile denoting a liking for a specific thing

ptero-, -pter relating to or having wings

quasi- apparently but not really; partly or almost

retro- denoting backward or reciprocal action; denoting location behind

-rrhea, -rrhoea, rheo- discharge, flow

rhodo-, rhod- roselike, rosy

sapro-, sapr- relating to putrefaction or decay

sarco-, sarc- of or relating to flesh

-sect, -section of cutting or dividing

-stasis, -static slowing down or stopping

steno- narrow

-ster denoting a person engaged in or associated with an activity or thing

stereo- of solid forms with three dimensions; of three-dimensional effect

strati-, strat- of or relating to layers or strata

sub- (suc-, suf-, etc.) lower; somewhat; secondary; supporting

super-, sur- above or beyond; to a great degree; extra large; of a higher kind

supra- above; beyond

syn-, sym-, syl- united; acting or considered together

tacho-, tachy- relating to speed; rapid

tauto- same

taxo-, taxi-, tax- of or relating to grouping or arranging

theo-, the- relating to God or to deities

thermo-, -therm, -thermy relating to heat

-tome denoting an instrument for cutting; denoting a section or fragment

topo-, top- of or relating to places or forms

-trix denoting a woman (where a man would be denoted by *-tor*)

-trophic relating to nutrition; relating to maintenance or regulation

-tropic, trop- turning toward; affecting; maintaining or regulating

ultra- beyond; extreme

ur- primitive, original, or earliest

vermi- relating to or like a worm

-vorous, -vore feeding on

xeno-, xen- relating to foreigners; other or different

xero-, xer- dry

xylo-, xyl- of or relating to wood

zoo- of animals; relating to animal life

zygo- relating to joining or pairing

A WEBLIOGRAPHY OF WEIRD AND WONDERFUL WORD SITES

The World Wide Web is well served by sites that feature the English language, especially its history and its peculiarities of vocabulary. Some of the better known and more popular ones are listed here. None concentrate exclusively on weird words, though they often form part of the mix.

MAILING LISTS

A Word a Day   <http://www.wordsmith.org/awad/subscribe.html>
Anu Garg's list is the granddaddy of online words mailing lists, now with more than half a million subscribers. A new word is sent out every weekday.

Merriam-Webster's Word of the Day
                    <http://www.m-w.com/service/subinst.htm>
A free seven-day-a-week service featuring a word, with a commentary, taken from the publisher's *Unabridged Dictionary.*

Vocabulary Mail   <http://www.vocabularymail.com>
A daily mailing, featuring anywhere from one to three words. The emphasis, again, is on building vocabulary.

Word of the Day   <http://www.dictionary.com/wordoftheday/list/>
Another seven-day-a-week service that is strongly biased toward vocabulary building, so usually features workaday words rather than weird ones.

Word Spy   <http://www.logophilia.com/WordSpy/subscribe.html>
Each weekday, Paul McFedries chooses a term culled from newspapers and magazines. The emphasis is on neologisms, so many of the choices reflect journalists' inventive wordsmithery.

World Wide Words   <http://www.worldwidewords.org/>
Michael Quinion writes on words from a British standpoint; his weekly e-mail newsletter is linked to a Web site, one of whose sections is actually called Weird Words ... Other regular dictionary definitions are featured on the *Oxford English Dictionary* and *AskOxford* sites—see below.

REGULAR WEB COLUMNS

OED Word of the Day   <http://www.oed.com/cgi/display/wotd>
Each daily word page consists of its full *Oxford English Dictionary* definition, with all its sub-senses and examples.

Take Our Word For It   <http://www.takeourword.com/>
Melanie & Mike discuss word etymologies, often of unusual, outmoded, or weird words. The site is updated weekly and you can get additional material and news of changes by joining a mailing list.

Word Detective   <http://www.word-detective.com/>
This is the Web archive of pieces on word history by Evan Morris which appear in his syndicated newspaper column. Updated every month.

Webliography

WRITINGS ON WORDS

Ask Oxford   <http://www.askoxford.com/>
A compendium of information about words, including Word of the Day, Quote of the Week, Ask the Experts, and word games.

Martha Barnette's Fun Words   <http://www.funwords.com/>
An entertaining compendium of quirky words.

Mavens' Word of the Day   <http://www.randomhouse.com/wotd/>
This has now closed, but an archive of past pieces gives answers to queries about the meanings of words and expressions.

Urban Legends Archive
          <http://www.urbanlegends.com/language/etymology/>
This discusses, and debunks, some of the stranger stories about the origins of words that circulate online and off.

Verbatim   <http://www.verbatimmag.com/>
The online archive for the quarterly magazine that investigates the (often odd) byways of language.

Word for Word   <http://plateaupress.com.au/wfw/articles.htm>
Articles on words and phrases by Australian writer Terry O'Connor.

Word Fugitives   <http://www.theatlantic.com/unbound/fugitives/>
Barbara Wallraff of the *Atlantic Monthly* features words that ought to exist but don't.

THE LOGOPHILE'S BIBLIOGRAPHY

A Selection of Oxford Dictionaries and Reference Works

DICTIONARIES

The Oxford English Dictionary. Second ed., twenty vols. 1989.

The 500-lb gorilla of the dictionary world, also available online by subscription at http://www.oed.com. Check with your local public library to see if they have a subscription for library cardholders available through the library website.

The New Shorter Oxford English Dictionary. Fifth ed., two vols. 2002.

Not just an abridgement of the twenty-volume *OED*, the *Shorter* has its own independent research program. With more than 83,000 quotations, this packs the punch of the *OED's* literary approach in a more manageable format. Also available on CD-ROM.

The New Oxford American Dictionary. 2001.

A completely new dictionary of American English from Oxford, with an innovative arrangement of definitions in which the more prominent core senses are given first, with related senses arranged in blocks underneath. This allows for a nice overview of constellations of meaning not possible with other dictionaries. Also available on CD-ROM.

The Oxford American Dictionary and Language Guide. 1999.

A very good general dictionary with a great deal of extra usage and language information, plus a 64-page reference supplement.

The Concise Oxford Dictionary. Tenth ed. 1999.

> The classic desk-size dictionary for British English, including the most current words and phrases and scientific and technical vocabulary. Word Formation features identify complex word groups such as *-phobias, -cultures,* and *-ariums.*

The Canadian Oxford Dictionary. 1998.

> The foremost authority on Canadian English, with more than 2,000 specifically Canadian words and senses, biographies of prominent Canadians, and more than 300 entries about Canadian aboriginal peoples and their cultures.

DICTIONARIES OF USAGE

Burchfield, R. W. *The New Fowler's Modern English Usage.* Third ed. 1996

> A completely revised and expanded version of the beloved *Modern English Usage* with examples from modern authors such as Tom Wolfe, Saul Bellow, and Iris Murdoch.

Fowler, H. W. *A Dictionary of Modern English Usage.* Second ed. 1983

> The most-beloved language reference book and the one by which all others are judged. And a darn good read!

Garner, Bryan. *A Dictionary of Modern American Usage.* 1998.

> The new authority for American usage and guidance not only for the grammar-impaired but for anyone who would like to write gracefully and precisely.

OTHER REFERENCE BOOKS

Ayto, John. *Twentieth Century Words.* 1999.

An overview of 5,000 words and meanings of the twentieth century, including *flapper, flower power,* and *road rage.*

Chantrell, Glynnis. *The Oxford Dictionary of Word Histories.* 2002.

This book describes the origins and sense development of over 11,000 words in the English language, with dates of the first recorded evidence from ongoing research for the *OED.*

Delahunty, Andrew, Sheila Dignan, and Penelope Stock. *The Oxford Dictionary of Allusions.* 2001.

A guide to allusions most frequently found in literature both modern and canonical. It covers classical myths and modern culture and ranges from "Ahab" to "Teflon," and "Eve" to "Darth Vader." Many entries include a quotation illustrating the allusion in use.

Greenbaum, Sidney. *The Oxford English Grammar.* 1996.

A complete overview of the subject, including a review of modern approaches to grammar and the interdependence of grammar and discourse, word-formation, punctuation, pronunciation, and spelling.

Knowles, Elizabeth, ed. *The Oxford Dictionary of Phrase and Fable.* 2000.
Drawn from folklore, history, mythology, philosophy, popular culture, religion, science, and technology, these alphabetically arranged entries include ancient gods and goddesses, biblical allusions, proverbial sayings, common phrases, fictional characters, geographical entities, and real people and events.

Lindberg, Christine. *The Oxford American Thesaurus of Current English.* 1999.
A great general thesaurus with an exclusive Writer's Toolkit and more than 350,000 synonyms.

Onions, C. T. *The Oxford Dictionary of English Etymology.* 1966.
The standard reference for scholars, this dictionary delves into the origins of more than 38,000 words.